WHERE *the* WORLD MEETS *to* PRAY

The Upper Room

WHERE *the* WORLD MEETS *to* PRAY

PEOPLE AND STORIES OF THE UPPER ROOM

MARY LOU REDDING

75 YEARS ANNIVERSARY EDITION

UPPER ROOM BOOKS®
NASHVILLE

This book is dedicated to the faithful people who worked on *The Upper Room* magazine in its early years whose names have been lost to us.

The Upper Room website: www.upperroom.org

Special thanks to Anne Trudel for her hard work in gathering many photos and other memorabilia used in this history. Thanks also to Dale Rust Waymack, Joan Floyd, Marilyn Beaty, Donna Bryant, Charlene Eubank, Frances Rivera, Carmen Gaud, Beth Richardson, Roland Rink, and Deen Thompson for their eager and cheerful assistance on this project. Much appreciation to Bruce Gore for going the extra mile.

Cover photo: Joe Pevahouse
Cover and interior design: Bruce Gore | www.GoreStudio.com

Library of Congress Cataloging-in-Publication Data

Redding, Mary Lou, 1950–
Where the world meets to pray : people and stories of The Upper Room / Mary Lou Redding.
p. cm.
"75th anniversary."
Includes bibliographical references.
ISBN 978-0-8358-9991-8
1. Upper Room (Publisher : Nashville, Tenn.) 2. Church work. 3. Fellowship. I. Title.
BV2370.U67R43 2009
267'.130973—dc22

2008055943

Printed in the United States of America

Contents

	Introduction	6
Chapter 1	The 1930s: People of Vision	9
Chapter 2	The 1940s: People Who Build	23
Chapter 3	The 1950s: People on the Move	41
Chapter 4	The 1960s: People Facing Change	53
Chapter 5	The 1970s: People Embracing the World	65
Chapter 6	The 1980s: People Willing to Risk	79
Chapter 7	The 1990s: People Taming Technology	93
Chapter 8	The New Millennium: People Welcoming the Digital Future	107
Epilogue	Still Listening	125
	About the Author	127

Introduction

The Upper Room magazine is about people. "That little book," as many identify it, has always been about people. In its pages, people from more than 100 countries—some that no longer even exist by the same names as appeared in the magazine—have spoken to one another. The meditations, written by people much like you and me, affirm a bedrock truth of the Christian faith: each of us has something to say to others about God's love and grace.

This book introduces and honors some of the people who have been a part of what God has been doing—for seventy-five years—through this daily devotional magazine and its worldwide ministry. Though I attempted to be scrupulous in confirming the details mentioned in these pages, this is not meant to be a scholarly history. Rather, I set out to tell the stories of some of the people who have invested themselves in *The Upper Room.*

The ministries that grew from the success of the magazine are part of the Christian witness of those men and women. I tried to work into this narrative the names of people I could identify as spending twenty years or more on the staff of the ministry. By their long tenure, such people inevitably shape the culture of their workplace so that it bears the imprint of their character and their lives. Of course I have missed some of these people—perhaps many. For this I apologize. The names of many who worked here in the early years have been lost; I regret that. Those people shaped the magazine and built its commitment to caring for our readers. *The Upper Room* would not be what it is today if they had not been part of it. So I mention people by name—honoring them as individuals—as a way to recognize all those who have been the backbone of the magazine day in and day out over the years.

When people learn that I work with *The Upper Room*, they often tell me their story of how the magazine has touched their lives. I love these stories. They remind me that *The Upper Room* occupies a privileged place in the lives of our readers. Through this magazine we sit with people at their breakfast table, speak to them in their bedrooms, travel with them on business and vacation, walk with them through the best and the worst experiences of their lives—and each day try to help them connect their story with God's story. But the magazine could not do that without the wonderful, honest, vulnerable people who write about their faith and allow us to publish their words. So we are back to where we started: *The Upper Room* is about people. I hope you will enjoy meeting some of them as you read this history.

The Upper Room is about people. Through this magazine we sit with people at their breakfast table, speak to them in their bedrooms, travel with them on business and vacation, walk with them through the best and worst experiences of their lives—and each day try to help them connect their story with God's story.

The vision

for the magazine was clear: to reestablish the "family altar" —the practice of daily prayer and Bible reading in individual homes.

THE 1930S: People of Vision

Chapter I

Though *The Upper Room* magazine began publication in 1935, we have to go back a bit earlier to pick up the strands of the story of the magazine's beginning.

The 1929 stock market crash brought on the Great Depression. The United States was in desperate straits, and church leaders encouraged believers to turn to God for help to make it through those difficult times. Some began talking about recovering the tradition of home worship, believing that faith was more critical than ever to help people hang on to hope that the future would be better.

In the late 1920s, Frances (Mrs. Seth A.) Craig worshiped and served at Travis Park Methodist Episcopal Church, South, in San Antonio, Texas. In her personal ministry with the ill and homebound, she saw the comfort people found in short devotional readings, and she urged her pastor, Dr. Paul Kern, to

Dr. Paul Kern's column "The Quiet Hour" in the *Travis Park News* inspired Frances Craig to pursue publication of a daily devotional booklet for a wider audience.

Travis Park News

The Official Organ of the Travis Park Methodist Episcopal Church, South

CORNER TRAVIS AND NAVARRO STREETS

PAUL B. KERN, D. D., Pastor

VOL. 8 SAN ANTONIO, TEXAS, MAY 19, 1929

2 TRAVIS PARK NEWS

TRAVIS PARK NEWS

Published each week by
THE BOARD OF STEWARDS
of the
TRAVIS PARK METHODIST CHURCH

Paul B. Kern, D.D., Pastor.............Editor-in-Chief
Mrs. Mary Beery
Mrs. A. A. Barber ....Associates
W. P. Cunningham, Associate Pastor.....Business Manager

Single Subscription mailed anywhere in the United States
$1.00 a Year...............$0.35 a Quarter
Advertising rate, $1.00 per inch each issue, pay- ... publication.

THE QUIET HOUR

A ROSARY OF KINGDOM PARABLES

Monday, May 20—
Matthew 13:31-32.

How encouraging is it that the emphasis of the kingdom is upon life and growth. It is not the size of the beginning, but beginning at all that matters. We have noted the solicitude of Jesus for the "smoking flax" for there is greater difference between absolute darkness and the tiniest challenging flicker, than between that speck of light and the perfected mazda. A right beginning finds the laws of growth with it and the resultant may give refuge to a world.

Frances Craig from Travis Park Methodist Episcopal Church, South, presented the idea of a daily devotional booklet to the Board of Home Missions, Evangelism, and Hospitals in 1934.

write a quarterly collection of short devotionals for their church. Though he could not find time for that, he did begin suggesting daily scripture readings in their weekly church newsletter. He included short notes a paragraph or so—to encourage his parishioners to read the Bible more regularly. Mrs. Craig became a champion of these notes. In fact, she encouraged Dr. Kern to publish and circulate them more widely, beyond Travis Park to the larger church. She kept talking to her pastor about helping people find a way to read the Bible and pray each day. When Paul Kern was elected bishop in 1930, his appointment ended the daily Bible-reading notes for Mrs. Craig and others at Travis Park. But Mrs. Craig did not forget the impact of that daily guidance in Bible reading.

Meanwhile, Grover Emmons, a clergyman of the Methodist Episcopal Church, South, was also being prepared for his future role in developing *The Upper Room*. Serving the church in France and in the Far East had engendered a world perspective in Emmons. Like many Christians who live as a minority outside the United States, he came to see that believers' common commitment to Christ is more important than denominational differences. This vision of the larger Christian community would shape a publishing work that would touch millions of lives. Upon his return to the United States, Emmons became a pastor. Somewhere along the way, he developed a dream of finding a way to help individuals and families "who wish to cultivate an acquaintance with God." He envisioned a devotional book that would be available and usable for all kinds of people.

Bishop Arthur J. Moore knew Grover Emmons and his skills, and when a vacancy occurred in the national staff of the denomination's Board of Home Missions, Evangelism, and Hospitals, Bishop Moore advocated for Emmons. So, in early 1934, Emmons came with his wife, daughter, and two sons to Nashville, Tennessee, site of the board, to work as secretary (director) of home missions, evangelism, and hospitals.

Frances Craig was also connected with the home missions board, serving as one of its volunteer directors on the Committee on Devotional Literature. In December 1934 when the board met, Grover Emmons (the staff person who worked with the committee) was called on to report about the committee's

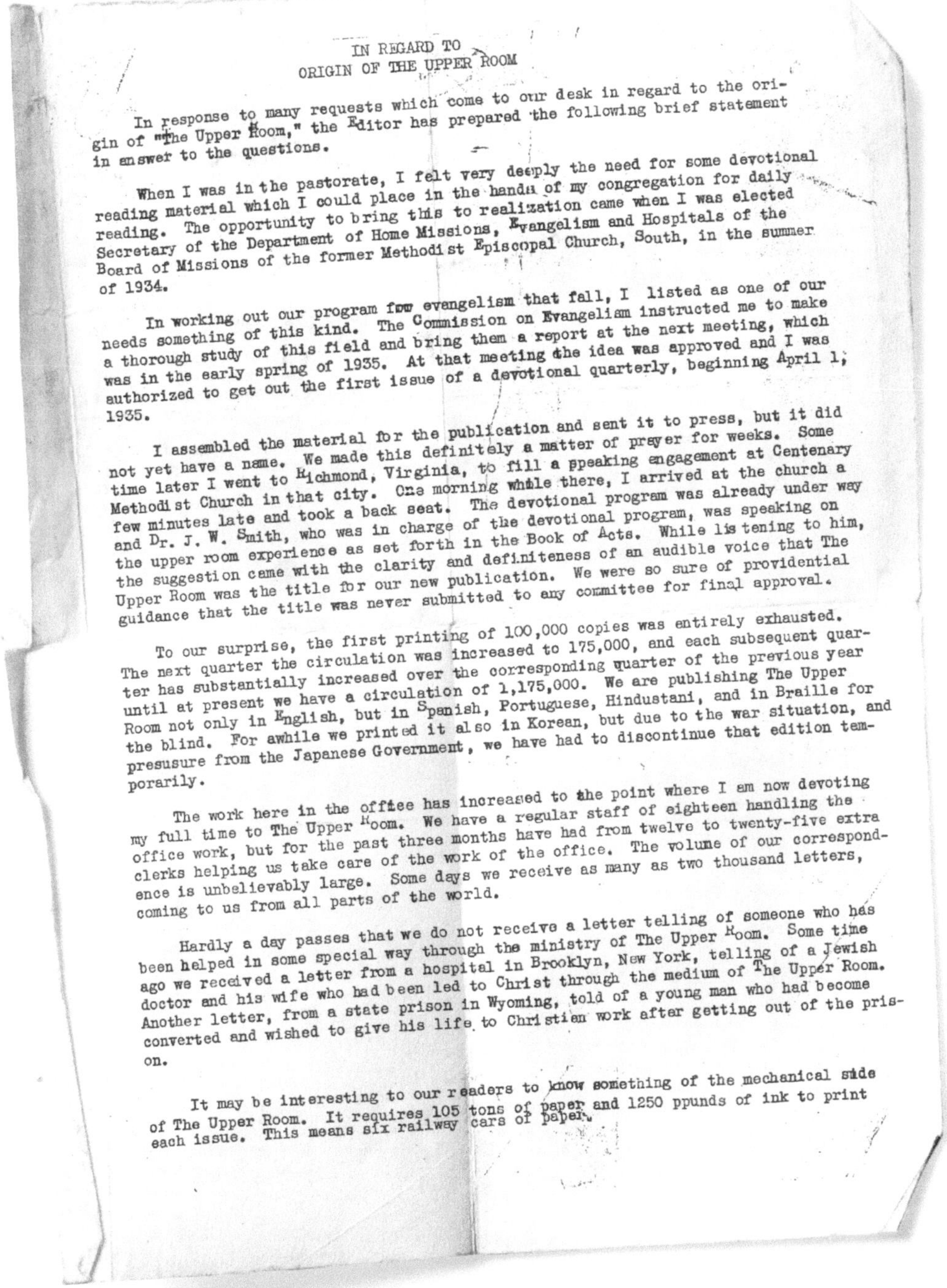

IN REGARD TO
ORIGIN OF THE UPPER ROOM

In response to many requests which come to our desk in regard to the ori-
gin of "The Upper Room," the Editor has prepared the following brief statement
in answer to the questions.

When I was in the pastorate, I felt very deeply the need for some devotional
reading material which I could place in the hands of my congregation for daily
reading. The opportunity to bring this to realization came when I was elected
Secretary of the Department of Home Missions, Evangelism and Hospitals of the
Board of Missions of the former Methodist Episcopal Church, South, in the summer
of 1934.

In working out our program for evangelism that fall, I listed as one of our
needs something of this kind. The Commission on Evangelism instructed me to make
a thorough study of this field and bring them a report at the next meeting, which
was in the early spring of 1935. At that meeting the idea was approved and I was
authorized to get out the first issue of a devotional quarterly, beginning April 1,
1935.

I assembled the material for the publication and sent it to press, but it did
not yet have a name. We made this definitely a matter of prayer for weeks. Some
time later I went to Richmond, Virginia, to fill a speaking engagement at Centenary
Methodist Church in that city. One morning while there, I arrived at the church a
few minutes late and took a back seat. The devotional program was already under way
and Dr. J. W. Smith, who was in charge of the devotional program, was speaking on
the upper room experience as set forth in the Book of Acts. While listening to him,
the suggestion came with the clarity and definiteness of an audible voice that The
Upper Room was the title for our new publication. We were so sure of providential
guidance that the title was never submitted to any committee for final approval.

To our surprise, the first printing of 100,000 copies was entirely exhausted.
The next quarter the circulation was increased to 175,000, and each subsequent quar-
ter has substantially increased over the corresponding quarter of the previous year
until at present we have a circulation of 1,175,000. We are publishing The Upper
Room not only in English, but in Spanish, Portuguese, Hindustani, and in Braille for
the blind. For awhile we printed it also in Korean, but due to the war situation, and
presusure from the Japanese Government, we have had to discontinue that edition tem-
porarily.

The work here in the office has increased to the point where I am now devoting
my full time to The Upper Room. We have a regular staff of eighteen handling the
office work, but for the past three months have had from twelve to twenty-five extra
clerks helping us take care of the work of the office. The volume of our correspond-
ence is unbelievably large. Some days we receive as many as two thousand letters,
coming to us from all parts of the world.

Hardly a day passes that we do not receive a letter telling of someone who has
been helped in some special way through the ministry of The Upper Room. Some time
ago we received a letter from a hospital in Brooklyn, New York, telling of a Jewish
doctor and his wife who had been led to Christ through the medium of The Upper Room.
Another letter, from a state prison in Wyoming, told of a young man who had become
converted and wished to give his life to Christian work after getting out of the pris-
on.

It may be interesting to our readers to know something of the mechanical side
of The Upper Room. It requires 105 tons of paper and 1250 ppunds of ink to print
each issue. This means six railway cars of paper.

Grover Emmons's notes on the beginning of *The Upper Room*

Travis Park Methodist Church in San Antonio was the birthplace of the idea for a quarterly devotional booklet.

work on "the matter of a publication for devotional use in the home." Mrs. Craig presented her idea for a quarterly booklet; two other ideas were also presented. The discussion produced no clear plan for how to proceed. Mrs. Craig and Dr. H. P. Myers (another volunteer board member) were added to the Devotional Life subcommittee. They, Dr. Emmons, and Dr. Burke Culpepper were directed to meet and bring a recommendation to the afternoon session of the board meeting. After lunch, in the board's 2:00 session, Mrs. Craig reported for the Committee on Devotional Literature, making this motion:

> . . . To publish a quarterly devotional booklet to be sold in the local church through the Missionary Committee and to bear the imprint of the Commission [on Home Missions, Hospitals, and Evangelism]. This is to be **an experiment for one quarter**, details to be referred to Dr. Emmons, Dr. [Elmer T.] Clark, Mrs. [J. W.] Downs, and Dr. [W. G.] Cram.

The board named Dr. Emmons to begin work on the devotional booklet—in addition to his already full-time duties as an executive for home missions and evangelism.

GROUNDED IN PRAYER

Above: Frances Craig asked the Philathea Sunday school class from Travis Park Methodist Church to make the new devotional booklet a "prayer special." We still describe the magazine as having been "prayed into existence."

Seeing the potential for such a magazine and believing deeply in the power of prayer, Mrs. Craig took the project back to Travis Park Methodist and marshaled her forces. She told the Philathea Sunday school class (a group of more than 100, which she taught) about the resolution and asked them to pray. Frances met weekly with a women's prayer group in the home of Bishop and Mrs. Arthur J. Moore in San Antonio. (Bishop Moore spent most of his time traveling.) Frances Craig asked these women also to pray for the work on the devotional guide. But she didn't stop there.

Dr. Grover C. Emmons, the first editor of *The Upper Room* (1935–1944)

She and Mrs. Moore also met with Mrs. L. L. Lentz, Mrs. W. E. Smith, and Mattie Lay (whom they called "Mother Lay") in a second weekly prayer group. Each Wednesday, the four younger women went to the Chandler Home for Women, where Mattie lived, to pray with and learn from her. This group also began praying for the devotional guide, making it, as Mrs. Craig wrote later, "our special prayer project." Frances Craig called Mother Lay "one of the most consecrated persons I have ever known." Mrs. Moore said later that she wished Mother Lay's picture could be placed somewhere in The Upper Room building because she felt that Mattie Lay's prayers, backing all the others, had a large part in the beginning of *The Upper Room.*

THE WORK BEGINS

Meanwhile, back in Nashville, Dr. Emmons spent evenings and weekends working on the devotional magazine. The pattern that evolved for the magazine's daily entries—a quoted scripture verse, a suggested scripture reading, brief comments, a prayer, and a closing thought for the day—is still used. But the format was not enough; a need for content still remained. Making a decision that would

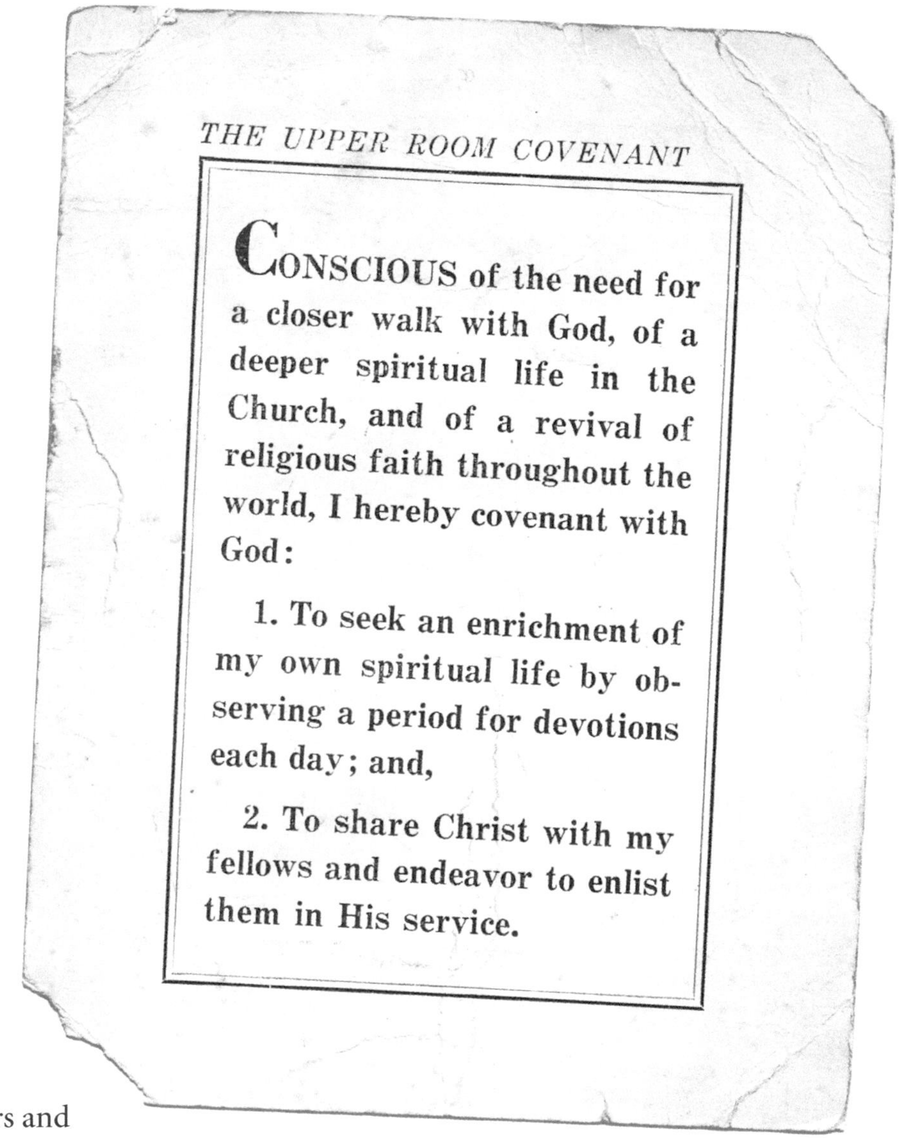

THE UPPER ROOM COVENANT

CONSCIOUS of the need for a closer walk with God, of a deeper spiritual life in the Church, and of a revival of religious faith throughout the world, I hereby covenant with God:

1. To seek an enrichment of my own spiritual life by observing a period for devotions each day; and,

2. To share Christ with my fellows and endeavor to enlist them in His service.

shape the magazine's unique emphasis on people, Emmons found a way to draw on the wisdom and experience of many: he invited individuals to write daily entries, beginning with those persons closest to the project. Several weeks after the board meeting, Frances Craig and Mrs. Arthur J. Moore received letters asking each of them to write two entries for the new magazine. This was their first indication that their prayers were having effect—production of the magazine was actually underway. In an amazingly short time, Dr. Emmons had the content for the first issue.

SPREADING THE VISION

While Grover Emmons worked on the first issues of the magazine, he and Bishop Moore traveled to evangelism meetings and conferences all over the United States, talking to pastors and other leaders about the new magazine. The vision for the magazine was clear: to reestablish the "family altar"—the practice of daily prayer and Bible reading in individual homes. The Upper Room Covenant, included in the early issues, expresses the spirit that underlies the magazine. (See this covenant on the previous page.)

From the beginning, Dr. Emmons and Bishop Moore reached beyond their own church to other Methodist groups and other denominations. The new magazine would not be just a Methodist publication but a gift from Methodists to the larger church. Drawing on his international experience and perspective, Dr. Emmons envisioned and created a devotional aid that was not doctrinaire but inclusive, centering not on differences that can divide believers but on beliefs that followers of Christ hold in common.

In early 1935, the first issue had been sent to the printer. In an amazing show of faith (some might say audacity), Emmons ordered a printing of 100,000 copies of the experimental issue, dated April-May-June 1935. The magazine was designed to be portable so that readers could carry their personal copy of the devotional guide with them. The magazine was sized to fit neatly in a man's inside vest pocket. What grew from a practical motive became a part of the magazine's identity as "that little book."

But, ready to go to press, the magazine still had no name. Attending a church conference in Richmond, Virginia, Grover Emmons found himself in worship at Centenary Methodist Church. As Reverend John W. Smith spoke about the power of God descending on Jesus' disciples as they prayed in an upper room, Dr. Emmons was inspired: the magazine would be called *The Upper Room*. This seemed a particularly appropriate name for a magazine meant to encourage

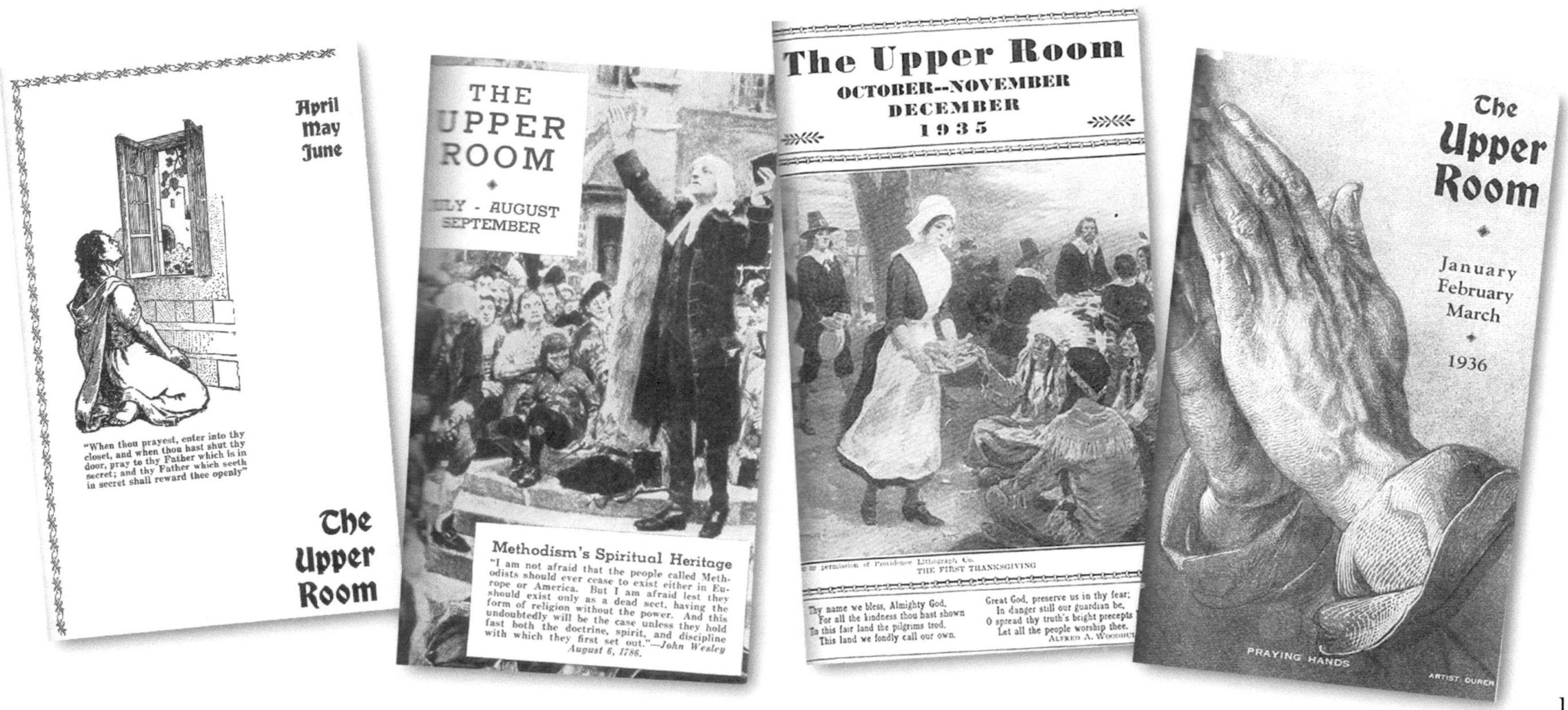

Covers of the first four issues of *The Upper Room*

Interpretations of the cover art, written by noted art commentator Albert E. Bailey, were included in *The Upper Room* starting in 1937. Cover art interpretations still appear in each issue.

readers to pray and connect with God's power in their individual "upper rooms." So sure was Dr. Emmons of the name that he didn't even ask the committee to respond. He sent a telegram to Nashville saying, "The name of the magazine is *The Upper Room*."

The first printing of 100,000 copies sold out immediately. Encouraged, the staff ordered 160,000 copies of the second ssue and 211,000 of the third issue. By the seventh issue, the rint run was 500,000—half a million copies. Beginning with e second issue, the Methodist Episcopal Church began cosponring the magazine, its name appearing along with the :thodist Episcopal Church, South, on the magazine's title page. The cover of the first issue featured a drawing of a believer at prayer. The next cover, and those since, featured religious art. Beginning in 1937, each issue also included a meditative interpretation of the art featured on the cover. Albert E. Bailey, a respected teacher and art commentator, wrote these interpretations. Use of religious art on its covers became an important part of *The Upper Room*'s distinctiveness—its brand identity.

Almost immediately after the magazine's publication, readers began sending in devotionals they had written that spoke of their faith. At first *The Upper Room* staff discouraged this. But soon they saw the value of including diverse voices and encouraging people to write about their faith. In 1938 the magazine began publishing meditations written by ordinary readers, not just invited writers. About seventy years before the phrase "user-generated content" came into our speech, *The Upper Room* embodied it, and the magazine's popularity affirmed its power.

As additional denominations endorsed the magazine for use by their members, circulation continued to rise. With the January–February–March 1939 issue, less than four years after the first copies rolled off the press, circulation reached an astounding one million copies per issue. The *little* devotional magazine was proving anything but small in its reach and impact.

MOVING OUTWARD

Reaching a circulation of one million was only the beginning. The magazine began to be distributed around the globe, translated into languages other than

The first editors of *El Aposento Alto* were Dr. Juan Pascoe and his wife, Elisa Strozzi de Pascoe. They worked on the magazine in Mexico City. Dr. Pascoe served as editor from 1938 to 1962. After his death, Elisa continued editing *El Aposento Alto* from 1962 to 1971. In 1971 the tasks of editing and producing the magazine moved to Nashville, Tennessee.

First issue of *El Aposento Alto*, the Spanish edition of *The Upper Room* and the translation in longest continuous publication

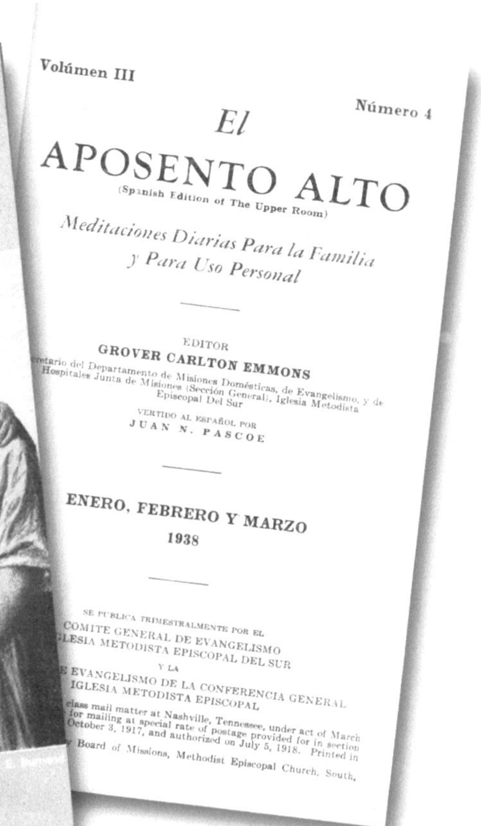

Volúmen III

Número 4

El

APOSENTO ALTO

(Spanish Edition of The Upper Room)

Meditaciones Diarias Para la Familia y Para Uso Personal

EDITOR

GROVER CARLTON EMMONS

etario del Departamento de Misiones Domésticas, de Evangelismo, y de Hospitales Junta de Misiones (Sección General), Iglesia Metodista Episcopal Del Sur

VERTIDO AL ESPAÑOL POR

JUAN N. PASCOE

ENERO, FEBRERO Y MARZO

1938

SE PUBLICA TRIMESTRALMENTE POR EL

COMITE GENERAL DE EVANGELISMO

LESIA METODISTA EPISCOPAL DEL SUR

Y LA

E EVANGELISMO DE LA CONFERENCIA GENERAL

IGLESIA METODISTA EPISCOPAL

class mail matter at Nashville, Tennessee, under act of March for mailing at special rate of postage provided for in section October 3, 1917, and authorized on July 5, 1918. Printed in Board of Missions, Methodist Episcopal Church, South,

English, and circulated outside the United States and Canada. The Korean, Spanish, and Hindustani translations began in 1938. The Spanish edition, *El Aposento Alto* (which literally means "The Upper Room"), is as of 2009 the translation in longest continuous publication. By 1939, the Spanish-language magazine was being distributed by agents within Argentina, Brazil, Chile, Cuba, Colombia, El Salvador, Korea, India, Mexico, and Puerto Rico. The phrase "worldwide fellowship" identified a network of people in many countries who were listening to one another through the pages of the magazine. This emerging community of believers stretched almost around the world.

We describe *The Upper Room* as having been "prayed into existence." And that is certainly true. James 5:16 tells us that the prayers of the righteous are "powerful and effective." Today's 2.5 million readers of the magazine in more than 100 countries are proof of the power of prayer that has undergirded *The Upper Room* since before its first pages were printed.

Decade Highlights

1934

Grover Emmons joins the staff of the (Methodist) Board of Home Missions, Evangelism, and Hospitals. Frances Craig presents idea for a quarterly devotional booklet to the board.

1935

The Upper Room begins publication.

1938

El Aposento Alto, the first other language edition, begins publication.

1939

One millionth copy of *The Upper Room* is printed.

In just fifteen years, the magazine grew to international prominence, linking people from around the world in a fellowship of daily prayer and Bible reading.

THE 1940S: People Who Build

Chapter 2

By the beginning of the 1940s, the name of the publisher of *The Upper Room* had changed. The Methodist Episcopal Church, South; the Methodist Episcopal Church; and the Methodist Protestant Church had united in 1939 to become the Methodist Church (USA).

Divided by the issue of slavery in the 1800s, these denominations' common heritage and practices drew them back together. The combined evangelism and mission agencies of the three denominations became the General Commission on Evangelism of the Methodist Church.

In the new structure, *The Upper Room* gained a tireless champion in the person of Harry Denman, executive of the commission. His work included overseeing the two publishing units: Tidings, which produced curriculum, tracts, and books specific to the Methodist Church; and The Upper Room, whose products served an interdenominational audience. Dr. Emmons's title in the new structure was coordinate general secretary of the General Commission on Evangelism. Another advocate for the devotional guide was Bishop Ralph Spaulding Cushman, one of those who oversaw the new commission.

Harry Denman addresses the committee of 200, which managed the Crusade for Christ of The United Methodist Church (1946).

A Pocket Prayer Book, by Bishop Ralph Spaulding Cushman, was an instant success. It sold millions of copies.

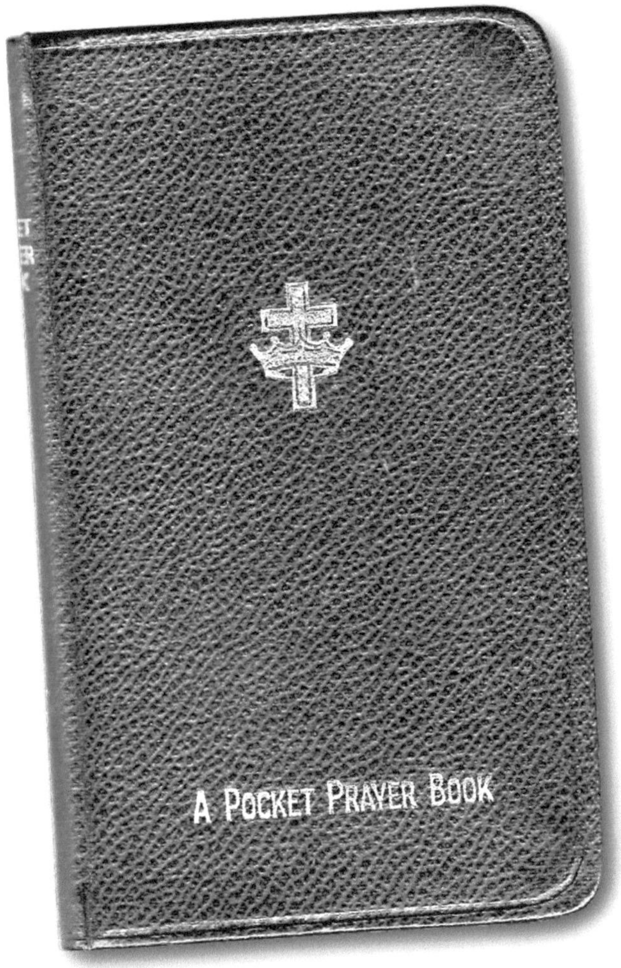

Bishop Cushman, a man of prayer, wholeheartedly supported the work of The Upper Room.

The world outside the church was also changing—in dramatic and disturbing ways. In reaction to Hitler's invasion of Poland in 1939, more and more countries entered World War II, and people of faith turned to God with prayers for peace. Dr. Emmons continued in his job as a director in evangelism ministries while gathering and training staff for the expanding publishing work. Lucy Kendall assisted in the work, handling operations in the Nashville office, while Dr. Emmons traveled, evangelizing.

Soon, readers of *The Upper Room* asked for more resources to help in devotion and daily prayer. In the spring of 1941, before the United States entered World War II, The Upper Room organization began publishing books. The first title, *Studies in Art*, was written by Dr. Albert E. Bailey, whose meditative art interpretations of covers of the magazine explored the symbolism of Christian art. Next came a little volume of prayers for various occasions. Compiled by Bishop Ralph Cushman, *A Pocket Prayer Book* met with instant success. This small book, about 3 by 5 inches, fit neatly into letters and greeting cards, purse or pocket. The black leatherette edition sold for thirty-five cents.

Upper left corner: Amy Proctor's meditation in the November–December 2008 issue of *The Upper Room*. **Small snapshot:** Ruth Chenoweth's parents, Otto and May Woods, picked up a copy of one of the first issues at their church in Glen Allen, Missouri (ghosted photo in background), in the 1930s. Their legacy of daily prayer and family Bible reading has continued for four generations. **Foreground:** Three successive generations of *Upper Room* readers (L to R): Andrea Proctor Brewer (Amy's sister), Amy Proctor, Mary "Jeannie" Proctor (Amy's mother), and Ruth Woods Chenoweth (Amy's grandmother, about whom she wrote her meditation).

Copies of *The Upper Room* cost five cents each; people picked up the magazine in their churches. Ruth Chenoweth recalls hearing about the magazine as a little girl in Missouri from a circuit-rider pastor. She decided the magazine must be really special to cost a whole nickel, and at the end of the service, she watched with surprise as her dad reached into his pocket for a coin to pay for

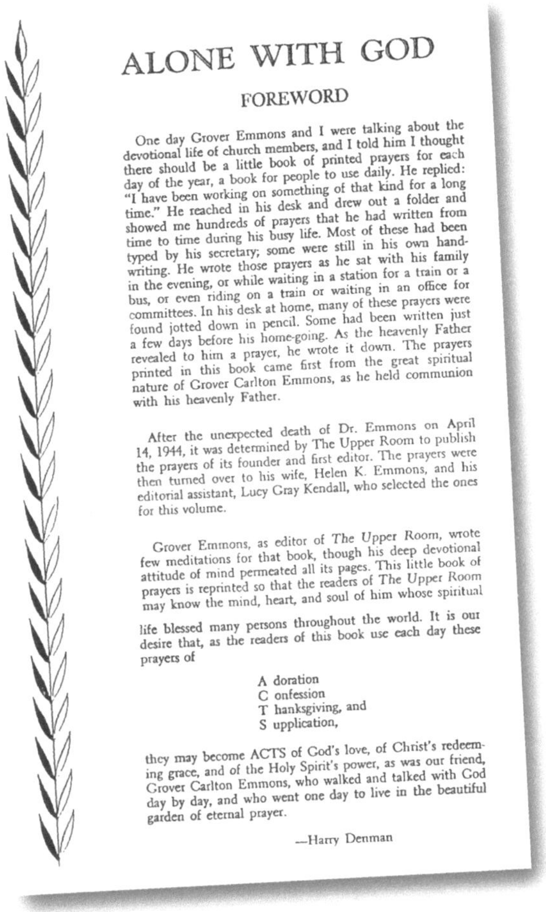

ALONE WITH GOD

FOREWORD

One day Grover Emmons and I were talking about the devotional life of church members, and I told him I thought there should be a little book of printed prayers for each day of the year, a book for people to use daily. He replied: "I have been working on something of that kind for a long time." He reached in his desk and drew out a folder and showed me hundreds of prayers that he had written from time to time during his busy life. Most of these had been typed by his secretary; some were still in his own handwriting. He wrote those prayers as he sat with his family in the evening, or while waiting in a station for a train or a bus, or even riding on a train or waiting in an office for committees. In his desk at home, many of these prayers were found jotted down in pencil. Some had been written just a few days before his home-going. As the heavenly Father revealed to him a prayer, he wrote it down. The prayers printed in this book came first from the great spiritual nature of Grover Carlton Emmons, as he held communion with his heavenly Father.

After the unexpected death of Dr. Emmons on April 14, 1944, it was determined by The Upper Room to publish the prayers of its founder and first editor. The prayers were then turned over to his wife, Helen K. Emmons, and his editorial assistant, Lucy Gray Kendall, who selected the ones for this volume.

Grover Emmons, as editor of *The Upper Room*, wrote few meditations for that book, though his deep devotional attitude of mind permeated all its pages. This little book of prayers is reprinted so that the readers of The Upper Room may know the mind, heart, and soul of him whose spiritual life blessed many persons throughout the world. It is our desire that, as the readers of this book use each day these prayers of

A doration
C onfession
T hanksgiving, and
S upplication,

they may become ACTS of God's love, of Christ's redeeming grace, and of the Holy Spirit's power, as was our friend, Grover Carlton Emmons, who walked and talked with God day by day, and who went one day to live in the beautiful garden of eternal prayer.

—Harry Denman

Harry Denman wrote the foreword to *Alone with God,* a book of prayers by Grover Emmons that was compiled and published after his death.

their family's first copy. Ruth's family used *The Upper Room* in family devotional time throughout her growing-up years, and she continued the pattern when she married and had children. (Ruth's granddaughter, Amy Proctor, wrote about her grandmother's spiritual influence on their family in a meditation published in the November–December 2008 issue of *The Upper Room.*)

NEW CHALLENGES

By 1942, the magazine's offices had moved to a new, larger building. A publication for pastors, *The Revival Pulpit,* was published by Tidings in 1944; in 1946 it was taken over by The Upper Room and renamed *The Upper Room Pulpit.* Each monthly issue included six sermons from leading preachers. Like *The Upper Room* magazine, this resource was deliberately interdenominational, using sermons from preachers in Presbyterian, Baptist, Congregationalist, Anglican, and other denominations.

As the war intensified, the staff worked with military chaplains to provide copies of the magazine to service personnel. While more copies of the magazine were needed, paper use was restricted. In 1943, all publishers in the United

States were required to reduce paper use by 10 percent. The Upper Room staff first met the challenge by reducing the weight of paper used for the magazine. Next, from July 1944 through March 1945, meditations were printed two per page. These smaller, lighter magazines also traveled cheaply by mail.

Countless copies of the magazine went to military personnel serving around the world. Mrs. W. M. Alexander, an enthusiastic Nashville friend of the magazine, also wrote meditations from time to time. She received a letter from a soldier who read one of her pieces while he served in Germany. Here is an excerpt from a letter she wrote about the experience:

> [*The Upper Room*] has been used in our family devotions and in my own personal quiet time. It has been my joy to send it to others—especially the boys overseas. [One soldier] wrote me a letter addressing it [only] to Mrs. W. M. Alexander, Tennessee, USA. On the envelope he wrote, "This may be opened for further information." He enclose[d] the page from the "Upper Room." In due time I received the letter. The letter had been opened and the page recognized and the letter sent to the "Upper Room" address in Nash[ville]

Samples from the July–September 1944 issue show the "Wartime Emergency" notice when paper use was restricted, a tribute to Grover Emmons, and a page of meditations printed two per page due to wartime paper restrictions

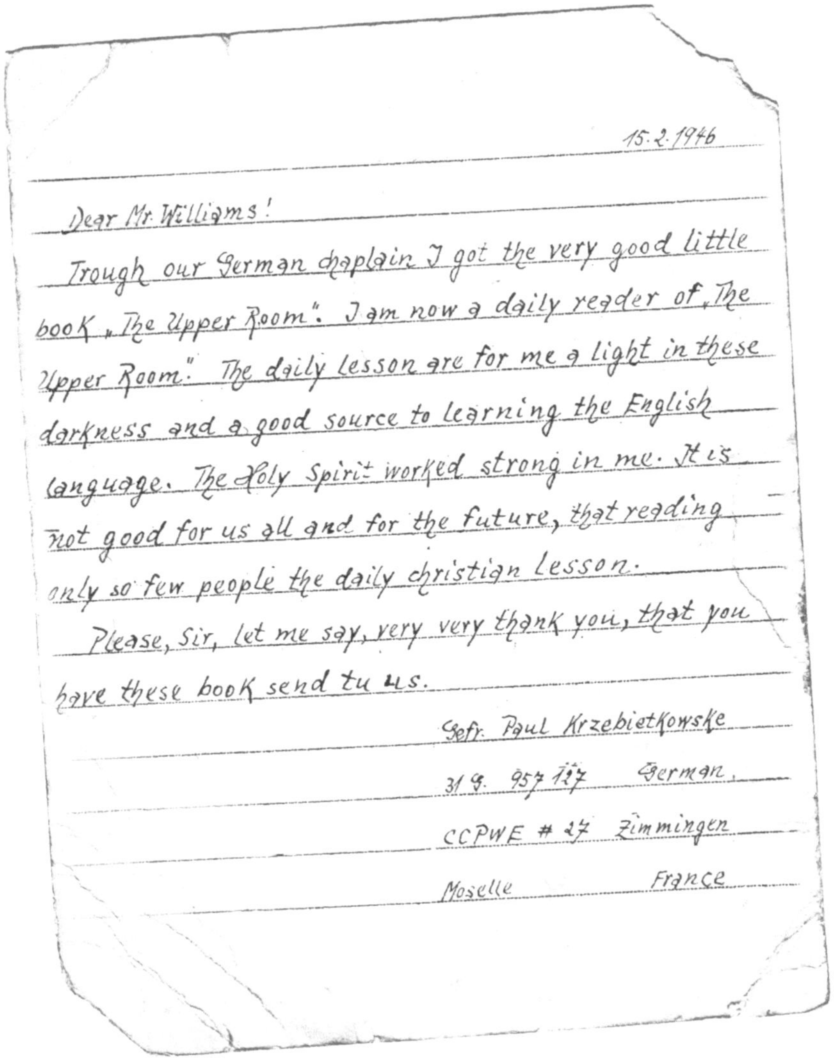

15.2.1946

Dear Mr. Williams!

Trough our German chaplain I got the very good little book „The Upper Room". I am now a daily reader of „The Upper Room". The daily lesson are for me a light in these darkness and a good source to learning the English language. The Holy Spirit worked strong in me. It is not good for us all and for the future, that reading only so few people the daily christian lesson.

Please, Sir, let me say, very very thank you, that you have these book send tu us.

Gefr. Paul Krzebietkowske
31 G. 957 127 German.
CCPWE # 27 Zimmingen
Moselle France

During World War II, the magazine was translated into German and distributed to prisoners of war. Above is a letter from a German prisoner of war.

> and sent on to me. In the letter the boy told me he was not a Christian and had never know[n] how to pray but he said, "The prayer you used in the meditation I have underst[oo]d and I am praying every day: Lord, for tomorrow and its needs I do not pray. Keep me, my God, from the stain of sin just for today. Amen." I wrote the boy, telling him where I had gotten the prayer. He wrote once again saying he had become a Christian and to please write his wife. I wrote to both of them again . . . I'm sure this story could be repeated many times.

Growth of the publishing work continued. By early 1943, Bishop Ralph Spaulding Cushman's *Pocket Prayer Book* had sold 197,697 copies. Sales of envelopes for mailing the military edition of *The Upper Room* totaled 254,625 in February of that year. Many more copies were tucked into letters and packages sent to those in the military. In 1943, the January–February–March printing of 1,716,000 copies sold out, and orders had to be refused. In 1944, a special undated issue of the magazine in German was printed for distribution to German prisoners of war.

A CHANGING OF THE GUARD

Grover Emmons's dream was reaching into literally millions of lives. In April 1944, after a week in Atlanta attending a meeting of the General Commission on Evangelism and a meeting of the Commission on Cooperation and Counsel of the Methodist Church (USA) and the Colored Methodist Episcopal Church, Dr. Emmons returned to Nashville. He took a rare day off, and late that afternoon, at home, he suffered a heart attack and died. *The Upper Room* staff, the Methodist Church, and Dr. Emmons's many friends in other denominations were stunned by the news of his sudden death. He was fifty-eight years old.

Messages of condolence came quickly from many countries, from every part of the United States, and from church leaders of various denominations. Many readers of *The Upper Room* also poured out expressions of sympathy. Here are a few that indicate the closeness readers felt (and still feel) to the magazine:

> *I . . . with many others, mourn the loss of a revered friend and wise counsellor, who, through The Upper Room, has won the esteem and confidence of a world-wide circle of friends.* —THOMAS MERRYWEATHER

Announcement of Grover Emmons's death that appeared in the *Nashville Banner*

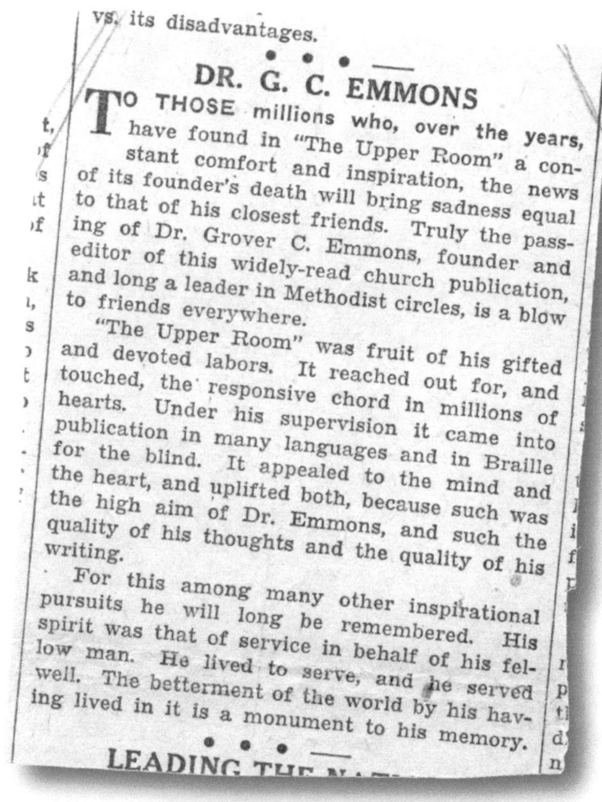

vs. its disadvantages.

• • •

DR. G. C. EMMONS

TO THOSE millions who, over the years, have found in "The Upper Room" a constant comfort and inspiration, the news of its founder's death will bring sadness equal to that of his closest friends. Truly the passing of Dr. Grover C. Emmons, founder and editor of this widely-read church publication, and long a leader in Methodist circles, is a blow to friends everywhere.

"The Upper Room" was fruit of his gifted and devoted labors. It reached out for, and touched, the responsive chord in millions of hearts. Under his supervision it came into publication in many languages and in Braille for the blind. It appealed to the mind and the heart, and uplifted both, because such was the high aim of Dr. Emmons, and such the quality of his thoughts and the quality of his writing.

For this among many other inspirational pursuits he will long be remembered. His spirit was that of service in behalf of his fellow man. He lived to serve, and he served well. The betterment of the world by his having lived in it is a monument to his memory.

• • •

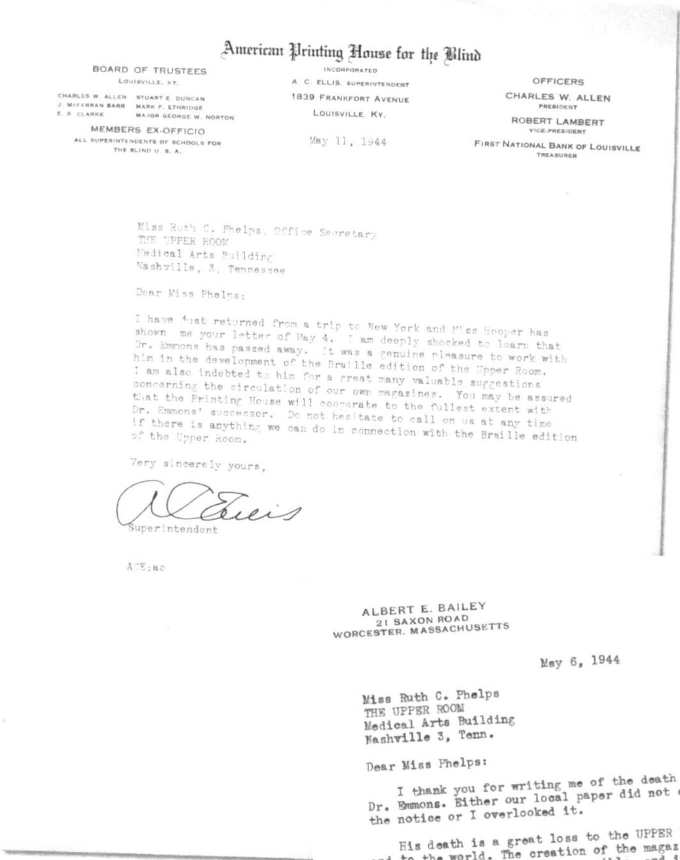

American Printing House for the Blind

BOARD OF TRUSTEES
LOUISVILLE, KY.
CHARLES W. ALLEN STUART E. DUNCAN
J. McFERRAN BARR MARK F. ETHRIDGE
E. B. CLARKE MAJOR GEORGE W. NORTON
MEMBERS EX-OFFICIO
ALL SUPERINTENDENTS OF SCHOOLS FOR THE BLIND U. S. A.

INCORPORATED
A. C. ELLIS, SUPERINTENDENT
1839 FRANKFORT AVENUE
LOUISVILLE, KY.

OFFICERS
CHARLES W. ALLEN
PRESIDENT
ROBERT LAMBERT
VICE-PRESIDENT
FIRST NATIONAL BANK OF LOUISVILLE
TREASURER

May 11, 1944

Miss Ruth C. Phelps, Office Secretary
THE UPPER ROOM
Medical Arts Building
Nashville, 3, Tennessee

Dear Miss Phelps:

I have just returned from a trip to New York and Miss Hooper has shown me your letter of May 4. I am deeply shocked to learn that Dr. Emmons has passed away. It was a genuine pleasure to work with him in the development of the Braille edition of the Upper Room. I am also indebted to him for a great many valuable suggestions concerning the circulation of our own magazines. You may be assured that the Printing House will cooperate to the fullest extent with Dr. Emmons' successor. Do not hesitate to call on us at any time if there is anything we can do in connection with the Braille edition of the Upper Room.

Very sincerely yours,

Superintendent

ACE:ac

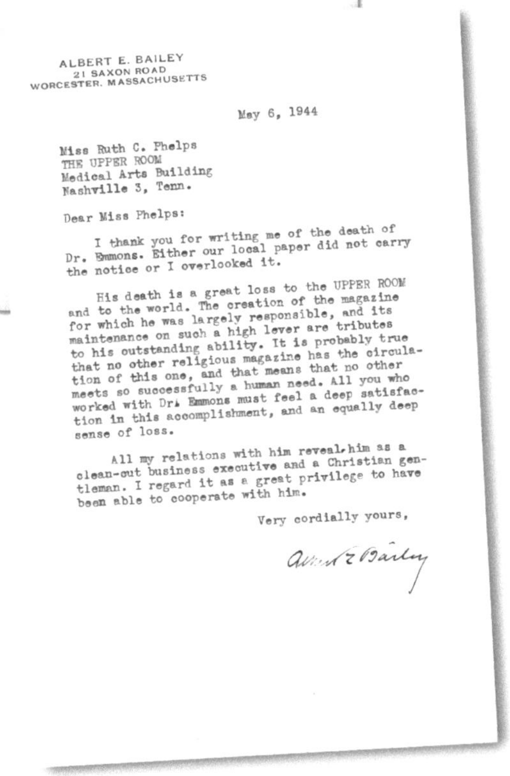

ALBERT E. BAILEY
21 SAXON ROAD
WORCESTER, MASSACHUSETTS

May 6, 1944

Miss Ruth C. Phelps
THE UPPER ROOM
Medical Arts Building
Nashville 3, Tenn.

Dear Miss Phelps:

I thank you for writing me of the death of Dr. Emmons. Either our local paper did not carry the notice or I overlooked it.

His death is a great loss to the UPPER ROOM
and to the world. The creation of the magazine
for which he was largely responsible, and its
maintenance on such a high lever are tributes
to his outstanding ability. It is probably true
that no other religious magazine has the circula-
tion of this one, and that means that no other
meets so successfully a human need. All you who
worked with Dr. Emmons must feel a deep satisfac-
tion in this accomplishment, and an equally deep
sense of loss.

All my relations with him reveal him as a
clean-cut business executive and a Christian gen-
tleman. I regard it as a great privilege to have
been able to cooperate with him.

Very cordially yours,

Letters of condolence poured into The Upper Room after Grover Emmons's death in April 1944. **Above** is one from the director of the American Printing House for the Blind; **to the right** is a letter from art commentator Albert E. Bailey.

The news of Dr. Emmons' death was a great shock to us. His creation of *__The Upper Room__* *was a piece of religious and Christian genius that met a need many of us had felt for a long time.* —O. H. LANGDON

Last night I was saddened and surprised to hear of Dr. Emmons' passing. Glad you accept and acknowledge *__The Upper Room__* *to be his monument. . . . Daily whenever I need guidance on any matter, on [*__*The Upper Room's*__*] pages my eyes fall on the exact message of cheer or warning or exhortation for that day, and I obey, knowing [God] makes no mistakes.*

—JOHN PRIDMORE

The meditation published for April 15, 1944, the day of Dr. Emmons's memorial service, was written by Wilson O. Weldon, of whom you will read more later. The quoted verse was Romans 14:8, KJV: "For whether we live, we live unto the Lord; and whether we die, we die unto the Lord: whether we live therefore, or die, we are the Lord's." The meditation offered a Christian view of death, saying, "Jesus gives both life and death a new look." It ended with a quote, "The tomb is not a blind alley. It is a thoroughfare. It closes on the twilight; it opens on the dawn."

A few weeks later Dr. Emmons's widow, Helen, wrote to Weldon:

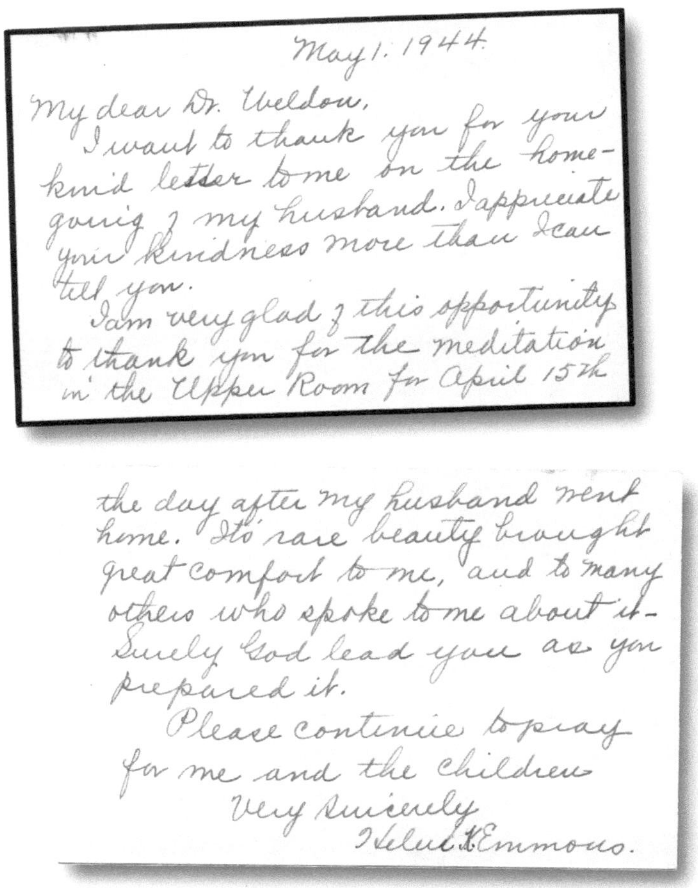

May 1. 1944.

My dear Dr. Weldon,
I want to thank you for your kind letter to me on the home-going of my husband. I appreciate your kindness more than I can tell you.
I am very glad of this opportunity to thank you for the meditation in the Upper Room for April 15th the day after my husband went home. Its rare beauty brought great comfort to me, and to many others who spoke to me about it. Surely God lead you as you prepared it.
Please continue to pray for me and the children
Very sincerely
Helen K. Emmons.

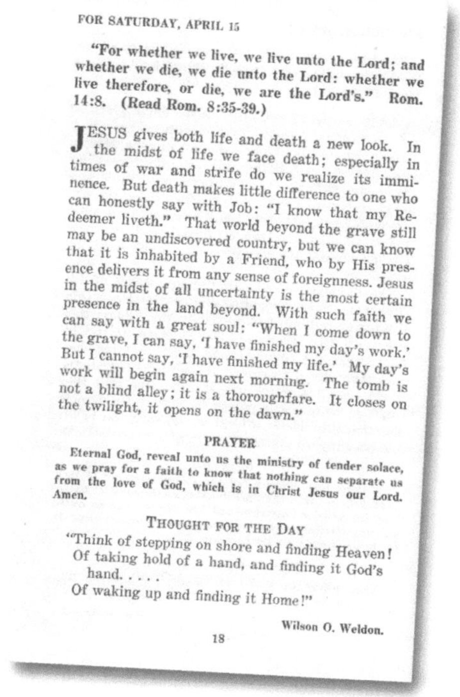

FOR SATURDAY, APRIL 15

"For whether we live, we live unto the Lord; and whether we die, we die unto the Lord: whether we live therefore, or die, we are the Lord's." Rom. 14:8. (Read Rom. 8:35-39.)

JESUS gives both life and death a new look. In the midst of life we face death; especially in times of war and strife do we realize its imminence. But death makes little difference to one who can honestly say with Job: "I know that my Redeemer liveth." That world beyond the grave still may be an undiscovered country, but we can know that it is inhabited by a Friend, who by His presence delivers it from any sense of foreignness. Jesus in the midst of all uncertainty is the most certain presence in the land beyond. With such faith we can say with a great soul: "When I come down to the grave, I can say, 'I have finished my day's work.' But I cannot say, 'I have finished my life.' My day's work will begin again next morning. The tomb is not a blind alley; it is a thoroughfare. It closes on the twilight, it opens on the dawn."

PRAYER

Eternal God, reveal unto us the ministry of tender solace, as we pray for a faith to know that nothing can separate us from the love of God, which is in Christ Jesus our Lord. Amen.

THOUGHT FOR THE DAY

"Think of stepping on shore and finding Heaven!
Of taking hold of a hand, and finding it God's hand. . . .
Of waking up and finding it Home!"

Wilson O. Weldon.

18

Wilson O. Weldon wrote *The Upper Room* meditation that appeared on the day of Grover Emmons's memorial service. Notice the theme for the day. Readers often comment about the timeliness of certain meditations for current events and for crises in their lives.

The magazine quickly became a tool for outreach. Pictured here is Mrs. Earl North reading a daily meditation to someone over the phone.

The magazine's readers often report a similar experience today—finding in the words of a believer perhaps half a world away guidance for living faithfully through a particular day's challenges. In 2008, after the state of Iowa endured devastating floods, a pastor returned to the damaged church and opened a copy of *The Upper Room* to that day's meditation. The quoted verse was Isaiah 43:2, "When you pass through the waters, I will be with you; . . . they shall not overwhelm you." The following Sunday she preached on that scripture verse. For her and her congregation, the words of that day's devotional became a message from God for their situation, for that day. The pastor said, "I know it was no accident. Though the work on that issue of the magazine was done months before, God was in it." God used Philip Polo, a bank accountant in Kenya who wrote that day's meditation, to speak a message of hope to a battered group of people thousands of miles away.

The Upper Room magazine is people—reaching out to one another, linked together by their common story of faith in Christ, learning from one another, and offering one another wisdom and comfort day by day.

EXPANDING THE MINISTRY

Lucy Kendall, Ruth Phelps, Harry Williams, Harry Denman, and others' names appear in the correspondence of the days following Dr. Emmons's death. Though Harry Denman traveled the world as an evangelist, he was quite familiar with the work of publishing the magazine. Under Dr. Denman's able leadership, the staff members trained by Dr. Emmons continued to publish the magazine while the search for a new editor began.

Dr. Roy Short, a Methodist clergyman and writer from Louisville, Kentucky, was soon chosen to succeed Dr. Emmons. The magazine had continued to set new circulation records during each of the war years, and Dr. Short came to a booming publishing enterprise—of not only the magazine but also books and tracts. In early 1946, the 50 millionth copy of *The Upper Room* came off the press. The "little" devotional guide was a publishing phenomenon unlike anything the church had seen.

Dr. Roy Short assumed leadership of *The Upper Room* after the sudden death of founding editor Grover Emmons. Dr. Short led the work of *The Upper Room* from 1944 to 1948.

Enju Hung presents a copy of an international edition to Dr. Roy Short, world editor.

But though the April–June 1946 issue went into all 48 states; Washington, DC; and 60 countries outside the United States, circulation overall was declining. The magazine also began to face competition as other denominations created their own devotional books. (Almost all were patterned after *The Upper Room*: small, in a daily format that included a Bible quote and a short meditation.) From the end of the war in 1945 through the end of 1946, circulation fell at the rate of 150,000 copies per issue. Circulation loss was unprecedented; for more than a decade, the magazine's print run had increased with every issue.

Dr. Short led efforts to find new ways both to promote the magazine and to support pastors in their work as spiritual leaders. Upper Room and evangelism staff worked together to strengthen commitment to home worship. The Christian Family movement, an emphasis of the General Commission on Evangelism, asked parents to attend Sunday school and church, engage in Christian conversation in the home, and read Christian literature as a family. The obvious usefulness of *The Upper Room* in this effort made cooperation natural and productive.

Work with military chaplains also continued. The Chaplains' Fund received donations and used the money to send copies of the magazine around the world.

Later this work merged with a new department, The Upper Room Fellowship, which Dr. Short created to provide copies of the magazine to institutions and individuals who could not afford to buy it. Readers grateful for their own copies gave generously to this effort.

The first entirely new venture, a radio ministry, grew from a vision of reaching every unchurched person in the United States with the gospel. Radio made it possible to think of going to every home in the country. On April 18, 1946, daily radio broadcasts of meditations from *The Upper Room* began. Shorter programs used just the thought for the day and a scripture verse. When these proved popular, programs including Christian music with the day's meditation were added, then dramatic programs that highlighted people struggling with spiritual questions. By 1949, more than 1,900 stations carried the program. Harry Williams, the business manager, became full-time director of the radio work, and The Upper Room Radio Parish was born. Dan E. Jackson joined the staff as business manager, a post he would fill for almost thirty years.

Dr. Short hired Harold Hermann as promotions manager. Dr. Short also hired the first person designated to do editorial work on *The Upper Room*:

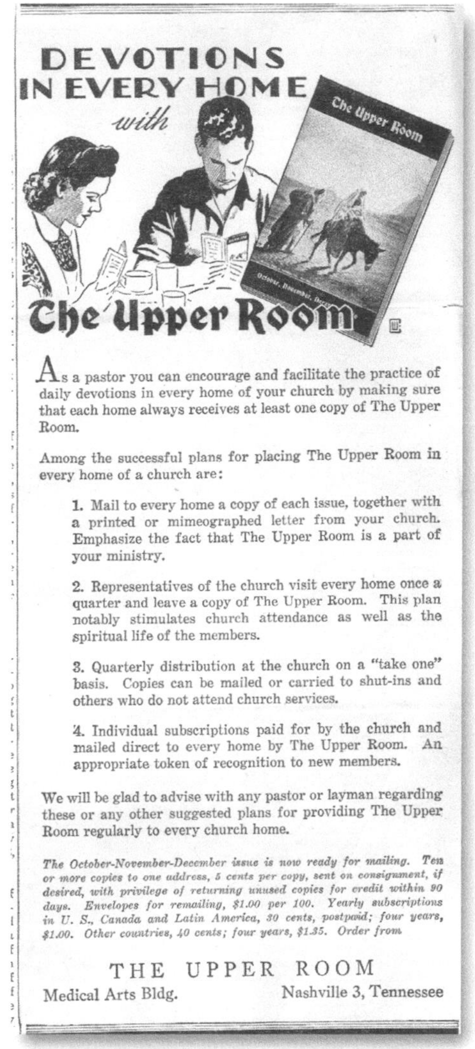

An ad in *News from The Upper Room*, 1946 shows *The Upper Room*'s support of the Christian Family movement, an emphasis of the General Commission on Evangelism.

Russell Q. Chilcote. Russ would stay with the magazine for twenty-eight years, shaping its content and eventually serving as managing editor.

By late 1947 the postwar circulation losses had been reversed, and the magazine was again printing record numbers of copies, going into millions of homes. Inevitably, those outside the organization saw a possibility for their own profit in the wide reach of the magazine. In 1947 someone offered an advertising contract that would pay $48,000 for their ads to appear in the magazine. That was a huge amount. Dr. Short, however, made a decision that still shapes the work of The Upper Room: he turned down the offer, saying that he refused to commercialize the ministry. To this day, though we continue to receive requests to do so, the magazine does not include outside ads. As the editors of many publications would attest, accepting advertising inevitably affects content.

The Upper Room's first home:
650 Doctors Building, Nashville, 1935–1941

A HOME OF ITS OWN

With the growth of the publishing work, *The Upper Room* needed more office space. Having started with no full-time employees in

Left, 166 8th Avenue, North, Nashville, 1942

Below, Medical Arts Building, Nashville, 1943–1947

1935, by 1945 the ministry employed almost fifty persons. As one account from that era put it, "It took fifteen girls just to open the mail." The too-small Medical Arts Building was sold, and in 1948, under Dr. Short and Dr. Denman's leadership, a parcel of land near Vanderbilt University was purchased as the site for a permanent home for this part of the church's work. The new structure would eventually house offices for both the Board of Evangelism and The Upper Room. D. E. Jackson and the business staff occupied the existing Victorian house on the land at the corner of 19th Avenue South and Grand Avenue, Nashville, Tennessee. Meanwhile, the shipping department moved to a house at the end of Laurel Street

Top: The building at 11th Avenue and Laurel Street, Nashville, where the yearly subscription and shipping departments were located from 1946 to 1952.

Middle: McGavock Street, Nashville. The accounting and treasurer's departments were housed here from 1950–1952.

Far right: The house at 1908 Grand Avenue, where the financial offices were located in 1947. The Upper Room Chapel now sits at the former location of this house.

Near right: The editorial staff worked in a fourth building, located on 18th Avenue South.

on 11th Avenue South. Offices of the General Board of Evangelism relocated to 2001 Division Street, and the editorial offices moved to 1022 18th Avenue South.

The irony of this venture was that the colorful Harry Denman, who never owned a home nor cared to do so in his adult life, helped lead the effort to give the Board of Evangelism and The Upper Room a permanent home.

MOVING OUTWARD

By the end of the 1940s, the magazine was published in English, Spanish, Portuguese, Braille (English), Chinese, Armenian, Tagalog and Ilocano (Philippine languages), Australian (English), and Korean editions. Within North America, the English edition of the magazine reached more than 50,000 churches of many denominations, including Presbyterian, Baptist, Christian, Lutheran, Moravian, Episcopal, and the Society of Friends (Quaker). The United Church of Canada officially endorsed *The Upper Room* for use by its members.

After Roy Short was elected bishop in 1948, Harry Denman again led the organization in searching for a new editor. It had been only four years since Grover Emmons's death, and many from the staff he trained carried on the publishing work. Named to succeed Roy Short was Dr. J. Manning Potts, who had most recently led the Methodist Crusade for Christ.

In just fifteen years, the magazine had grown to international prominence, linking people from around the world in a fellowship of daily prayer and Bible reading.

Dr. J. Manning Potts was named editor of *The Upper Room* when Dr. Roy Short was elected as a bishop in the Methodist Church.

Decade Highlights

1940

Braille edition of *The Upper Room* begins.

Chaplains begin distributing magazine to the military.

1941

A Pocket Prayer Book by Ralph Spaulding Cushman is published.

1944

Dr. Grover Emmons dies; Dr. Roy Short is elected editor.

1946

Fifty millionth copy of *The Upper Room* is printed.

The Upper Room Radio Parish is established.

1948

Dr. Roy Short is elected bishop; Dr. J. Manning Potts becomes editor.

1949

Full-color art covers begin.

First Upper Room Citation is awarded.

Potts and Denman were both deeply committed to Christian fellowship across national, denominational, and racial lines.

THE 1950S: People on the Move

Chapter 3

The postwar baby boom that filled U. S. schools also filled growing churches. *The Upper Room* magazine grew too, not just in the United States but also around the world. By January 1950, the magazine was published in 30 languages, and the international, interdenominational vision of its leaders promised more growth to come.

The 1950s were the era of the family, and many Methodist churches observed National Family Week, an emphasis of the General Commission on Evangelism. The Methodist Church urged its pastors and leaders to model prayer and devotional life and recommended *The Upper Room* magazine widely as an important tool for family worship time. The May–June 1951 issue set a circulation record of 2.3 million copies. Circulation would continue to climb through the decade.

But in the midst of national emphasis on the home, *The Upper Room* had no home of its own. The publishing operation had outgrown several buildings, and as the 1950s began,

The completion of The Upper Room Chapel, featuring a carved wood reproduction of Leonardo da Vinci's *Last Supper*, was a highlight of the 1950s.

During the early 1950s, construction began on a building for *The Upper Room*. Finally the magazine would have a home of its own.

the editorial, shipping, and business operations were housed in four different locations. Acting for The Upper Room and the General Board of Evangelism, Methodist leaders had purchased land at 1902, 1904, 1906, and 1908 Grand Avenue in the late 1940s. As previously mentioned, D. E. Jackson and the business staff occupied the Victorian house on that parcel of land. Jackson, Roy Short (by this time Bishop Short), Harry Denman, and the new editor, J. Manning Potts, were on the building committee that began meeting in April 1950. They directed the architects to design a headquarters building with a chapel at its center, a chapel that would reflect the character of *The Upper Room* magazine. In 1951, Potts wrote in *The Upper Room: A Devotional Shrine* that the chapel's symbolism was to "demonstrate visually to the worshipers here the art which we have been talking about and to speak to them of eternal things through the medium of ordinary objects in the run of the day's experience." (Speaking of the eternal through the ordinary also describes the meditations in the magazine.) The chapel would feature art as a focal point. The committee considered three media: oil, glass, or wood. The subject of the art would be Jesus' Last Supper with his disciples in an upper room. The committee settled on wood as the medium and chose the D'Ascenzo firm of Philadelphia to create the art.

The piece was to be a recreation of Leonardo da Vinci's famous painting *The Last Supper*. Groundbreaking for the building took place on March 5, 1952, with the chapel scheduled to open in May 1953.

Sculptor Ernest Pellegrini directed the three-dimensional re-creation of da Vinci's famous painting; the chapel's altar area and walls echo the tapestry and table in the painting. The massive wood carving is seventeen feet wide by eight feet high. Though it gives the illusion of great depth, actually it is only eight inches deep at its extreme. Yet the figures in the scene seem to reach out into the chapel. The beautiful carving immediately became an attraction for people visiting Nashville. Within two years of the chapel's opening, almost 71,000 guests had admired its beauty. The building at 1908 Grand Avenue was described as the only building in the church devoted entirely to prayer, the devotional life, and evangelism.

In addition to offices and a shipping facility, the new building also featured a museum and a library. The library included many classics of devotional writing and housed the archives of the publishing arm of the ministry. The museum collection reflected the worldwide reach of *The Upper Room* magazine.

MATERIALS PLACED IN THE CORNERSTONE

The Bible • *The Discipline* • *The Christian Advocate* • *The Circuit Rider* • *Evidence*, yearbook of the Board of Evangelism • *Shepherds*, vol. 1, no. 1 and vol. 6, no. 6 • pictures of the board and staff • List of the staff and employees • catalog of Scarritt College • newspapers • *The Upper Room*, vol. 1, no. 1; May–June 1952 issue; these editions: pocket; Braille; Australian; Indian; Hindi; Japanese; Korean; Chinese; Greek; German; Portuguese; Swedish; Spanish; Armenian; Tagalog; Ilocano; Norwegian; Italian; Hindustani; *The Upper Room Pulpit*; a recording of The Upper Room Radio Parish; Upper Room publications: *The Upper Room Chapel*; *Alone with God* by Grover C. Emmons; *A Pocket Prayer Book* by Ralph S. Cushman; several other books; Tidings publications: *The Methodist Primer* by Charles C. Selecman; *Essentials of Evangelism*, Ralph S. Cushman; *Evangelistic Preaching*, Roy H. Short, and many others.

The Upper Room Chapel quickly became a tourist attraction for visitors to Nashville.

During his travels, Dr. Potts received gifts from many hosts; most of these objects found their way into the museum. Over the years, other editors of the magazine have sent or brought back pieces of art and symbols of Christian faith representing the cultures of our partners on other continents. Crèches given by a few of our international friends became the seed for a collection of nativity sets from dozens of countries, in dozens of styles. Each Advent, a display of these crèches draws visitors to the museum.

From ornate and expensive crèches to simple ones made of common materials such as straw, the crèches reflect a bit of the amazing diversity and talent of God's people. Displaying them honors our partners around the world and delights guests. Because the collection includes so many crèches, not all can be displayed at one time, making the exhibit unique from year to year.

A final feature, the World Christian Fellowship Window, completed the chapel. This twenty-foot-tall stained-glass window celebrates the Christian fellowship at the heart

Nativity sets from countries around the world have been displayed in The Upper Room Museum. Many of the crèches were given to The Upper Room by its international publishing partners.

The Pentecost Window, later renamed the World Christian Fellowship Window, is one feature of The Upper Room Chapel that has inspired visitors since its installation in 1959. The window is 20 feet high and contains four central medallions that tell the story of the Day of Pentecost. Along the edge of the window are depictions of heroes of the faith through the centuries.

Harry Denman preaches at a tent revival in 1955.

of worldwide ministry and links the upper room of the Last Supper with the upper room where 120 disciples were filled with the Holy Spirit on Pentecost. Dedicated in 1959, the window depicts Bible characters and leaders of many Christian groups, as well as leaders in devotional life.

A HOME FOR HARRY

One of the champions for building a home for this ministry, Harry Denman, traveled the world as an evangelist for the Methodist Church. Often he was accompanied by Manning Potts as Dr. Potts cultivated international partnerships on behalf of *The Upper Room*. Harry seldom slept in Nashville more than a few nights in a month—so few that he hardly used the apartment he rented in a building near 1908 Grand. Knowing this, the building committee insisted on one unusual feature for the new building: living quarters for Harry. On the second floor, behind his office, Harry Denman had a small apartment. From 1953 on he made the building where he worked his home.

Harry was quite a character, famous for traveling with two briefcases—and no other luggage. In one briefcase he carried his Bible, sermons and talks in progress for upcoming engagements, and writing materials. (Harry wrote literally thousands of letters, corresponding over many years with the friends he made in his world travels.) In the second briefcase he carried a few extra shirts, his pajamas, underwear, and toiletries. With this small kit he covered hundreds of thousands of miles.

While the chapel and headquarters were being built, the publishing work continued and grew. The Upper Room published two well-received aids to family practice of holy habits: *Table Graces from The Upper Room* and *Prayers from The Upper Room.* The small *Pocket Prayer Book* by Ralph S. Cushman also continued to sell many copies. Through The Upper Room Fellowship, work with military chaplains continued. Gifts of magazines to institutions and to persons who could not afford to pay were coordinated through the fellowship office.

In 1953 Mary Ann White came to work with the fellowship department. For more than forty years, she responded to letters asking for prayer and for

Manning Potts and Harry Denman became the face of *The Upper Room* as they traveled around the world promoting evangelism and the devotional life.

copies of the magazine, and she handled requests from the staffs of editions outside the United States. Over the years, directors of the fellowship department came and went, but Mary Ann's presence remained constant. For the recipients of her gentle and compassionate responses, Mary Ann represented the caring presence of the ministry. She signed letters for the fellowship department with the word *Fellowship* followed by a slash and her initials, MAW. In 1975 when editors from around the world gathered in Nashville to celebrate the magazine's fortieth anniversary, a delegation told their hosts that one person they must meet was "Fellowship Maw." Christians in other countries even named their children "Fellowship" to recognize the consistently caring spirit reflected in the letters they received. "Fellowship" described well Mary Ann's function; building relationships was her gift. Embodying the claim that *The Upper Room* is about people, she honored and loved staff members and readers alike. (See Mary Ann's photo on page 111.)

Miss Mary Watkin, Mrs. Mamie Snapp, and Mrs. Katherine Hill, employees of Parthenon Printing in Nashville, read proofs of the magazine.

At right, Dr. J. Manning Potts, world editor, receives from Reuel Buchanan the first copy of the new "Talking Book" edition of the daily devotional guide.
Below, Tina Lou Wallace, editor of the Talking Book edition

MINISTRY ON THE MOVE

The broadcasting ministry also grew during the 1950s. The Upper Room Radio/TV Parish produced programs in a variety of formats. Longer radio programs included readings of meditations from the magazine accompanied by instrumental versions of hymns and vocal music. An Upper Room radio choir was created and featured in many of the programs. The "Thought for the Day" twenty-second radio format aired on 2,138 stations, and the meditation for the day aired on more than a thousand stations from 1956–1960. A new employee of the radio parish in 1955, Mary Ruth Coffman, had recently returned to the United States after serving in South America as a missionary. She joined the staff as a secretary, but Dr. Potts recognized and rewarded potential. Even before the sweeping social changes of the 1960s, he championed and promoted women. Mary Ruth soon moved into a professional role in the department. (See page 59 for a picture of Mary Ruth.)

In 1957 the Talking Book edition of *The Upper Room* was launched. Recordings of the daily meditations on long-playing vinyl records allowed people with visual impairment to join readers around the world in a daily time with God.

The ministry to military personnel that began in the 1940s continued in the 1950s as *The Upper Room* was distributed during the Korean War. **On the immediate right,** a chaplain distributes copies of the magazine in Korean to personnel along the front lines. **To the far right,** four military men read their copies of *The Upper Room* in Korean.

In 1958 the radio ministry received a Freedoms Foundation medal for its Holy Week radio series "Seven Last Words." Radio broadcasts totaled 338,010 in the first ten months of 1959.

Manning Potts and Harry Denman were both deeply committed to Christian fellowship across national, denominational, and racial lines. In the 1950s, The Upper Room established the annual Upper Room Citation, given to recognize someone who had significantly advanced Christian fellowship. Publishing *The Upper Room* around the world was possible because of fellowship and cooperation with both denominational and interdenominational groups, and awarding the citation honored those who demonstrated the values that had allowed *The Upper Room* magazine to grow.

Dr. Manning Potts presents Warner Sallman with The Upper Room Citation in 1957. In the background is Sallman's famous painting of Christ.

By the end of this decade, the magazine had expanded to 37 editions, thanks to the work of J. Manning Potts, who built partnerships around the world. *The Upper Room* continued to extend its ministry within the United States as well, setting one circulation record after another. The 1950s were a time of tremendous growth—and more was yet to come.

In the late 1950s a major part of the magazine's ministry was its radio outreach. Shown here are Eric Lund, program director for station WLVA in Lynchburg, Virginia, and Harold Hermann, publicity director for The Upper Room. Vinyl records were the means for distributing *The Upper Room* as a "Talking Book" edition.

Decade Highlights

1951

100 millionth copy of *The Upper Room* is printed.

1952

A Pocket Prayer Book reaches one million copies.

1953

The Upper Room Chapel opens.

1954

Number of editions reaches 27.

1957

Talking Book edition begins.

1958

Pocket books—*Prayer, Faith, Power,* and *Hope*—reach a total of two million copies.

The Upper Room receives Freedoms Foundation at Valley Forge award.

1959

250 millionth copy of *The Upper Room* is printed.

World Christian Fellowship Window in The Upper Room Chapel is dedicated.

The magazine began the decade with 37 editions; by 1967, the number of editions had grown to 45, in 31 languages.

THE 1960S: People Facing Change

Chapter 4

In April 1960, the Methodist Church met in Denver for its General Conference, the assembly of Methodists that occurs every four years. During the conference, delegates attending from around the world gathered with U.S. delegates to celebrate the twenty-fifth anniversary of *The Upper Room* magazine. Telegrams, letters, and notes of congratulation came from Christian groups on several continents and from representatives of a dozen denominations in the United States.

Perhaps the most memorable is a handwritten note from Helen Emmons, widow of the magazine's creator, Grover Emmons. She said, "From its beginning [the magazine] has been led of God and has met a profound need. Each succeeding year and leadership has brought to it new vision and greater accomplishment. We say with one of old, 'What hath God wrought!'"

When you consider that the circulation of *The Upper Room* would exceed 3.25 million later in the decade, her words seem apt. God had taken the "little"

Harry Denman and Bishop W. Angie Smith with the Warner Sallman portrait of Denman presented at the Board of Evangelism meeting, 1964.

magazine far beyond Travis Park Methodist Episcopal Church, South, beyond the Methodist denomination's boards and agencies, beyond its international work, to readers of many denominations on many continents. Who would ever have predicted all this?

Much of the magazine's expansion in the 1960s grew from the work of the editor, Dr. Manning Potts, and Harry Denman. These two men shared a vision of Christians from many nations around the world joined by a deep commitment to prayer. To move their dream from vision to reality, Manning and Harry traveled to many countries, often together.

The eccentric Harry Denman owned one suit, saying that he could wear only one at a time, so why own more? Yet Harry was also scrupulous about personal cleanliness. So during his travels, he often sent his suit to be cleaned by the hotel service after checking in for the night. Usually his suit would be back by the time he needed it. At least once, however, it did not arrive as expected.

The Reverend Billy Graham received The Upper Room Citation, an award to recognize outstanding contributions to worldwide Christian fellowship, in 1964. Shown here with Rev. Graham is Dr. Norman Vincent Peale, who attended the citation award dinner.

After traveling with Manning to India, Harry sent the suit to be cleaned and pressed after they checked into the hotel. When the time came to meet colleagues for dinner, Harry's only pair of pants had not been returned. Ever resourceful, Harry had an idea: he would borrow pants from Dr. Potts. The thin Harry towered over the portly Dr. Potts, who was at least six inches shorter than Harry. That difference did not matter to Harry. He came down to dinner with no coat, wearing Manning's trousers held up by suspenders, the too-short pants legs showing the tops of Harry's socks. Obviously the two were close friends. In a report on his visit (alone) to Sweden and Norway in June 1963, Harry wrote,

> I certainly miss my good friend and traveling companion Manning Potts. He is so good to overlook my weaknesses when we travel together, and now I am having to take it all out on myself, which is hard on me. It is lots of fun to travel with Manning. I would rather travel with him than with me.

The shared vision of these men—of Christians in many countries bound together by prayer—led to the creation of the World Christian Fellowship. The

In the 1960s the magazine moved to reach people around the world. Here four Portuguese fishermen are shown reading *No Cenáculo*, the Portuguese edition of *The Upper Room*, onshore at St. John's, Newfoundland, in 1964.

Upper Room cosponsored an International Prayer Fellowship conference at Ewha Womans University in Seoul, Korea. The next year, the conference met in Nashville. A brochure for a meeting of the International Prayer Fellowship bore the phrase *International, Interdenominational, Interracial.* Shortly afterward, these descriptors were added to the title page of *The Upper Room* magazine. They still appear in each issue.

The magazine began the decade with 37 editions. By 1967, the number of editions had grown to 45, in 31 languages. This expansion came about primarily because of Dr. Potts; as he traveled, he eagerly sought persons who were committed to daily prayer and reflection on the Bible. Then he established relationships that often led to new editions of the magazine.

MEANWHILE, BACK AT THE RANCH

In addition to international work, The Upper Room also turned attention to Christian leaders here at home. *The Upper Room Pulpit*, published for pastors, collected outstanding sermons from preachers of various denominations. Though their subjects followed the Christian calendar in addressing Lent, Advent, and other special emphases, each volume was self-contained. Beginning in the 1950s, *The Upper Room* magazine organized daily entries around weekly themes. Then Dr. Potts and Harold Hermann decided to create a yearly devotional book for leaders called *The Upper Room Companion*, mirroring the magazine's weekly subjects. Described as a resource "for theological students, professors, ministers, chaplains, and professional workers in the church," the *Companion*'s invited writers addressed these themes, delving

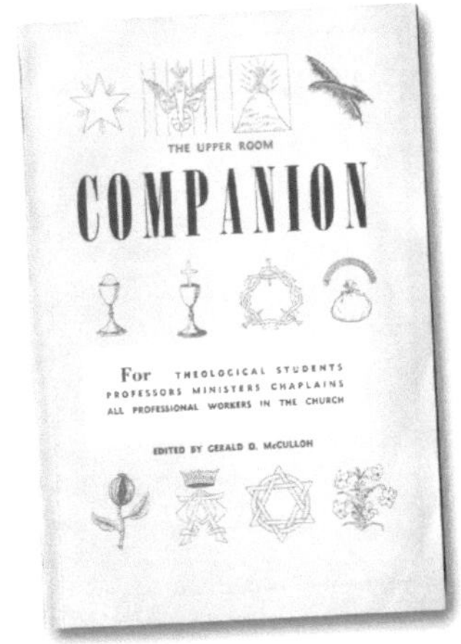

The Upper Room Companion debuted in 1959 and contained devotions that paralleled selections in *The Upper Room.* In 1960 *The Upper Room Companion* was renamed *The Upper Room Disciplines* to encourage ministers and other servants to practice "the spiritual discipline of the daily practice of the presence of God."

The 50th anniversary edition of *The Upper Room Disciplines* (2009)

more deeply into them by preparing daily readings for an entire week. The yearly plan allowed leaders to look ahead to the subjects they and their members would be reading about in their daily devotional times. The *Companion* built on the vital spiritual disciplines of daily Bible reading and prayer. In 1961, to reflect this emphasis, the name was changed to *The Upper Room Disciplines*. The weekly meditations in *Disciplines* are now based on the Sunday readings from the *Revised Common Lectionary*. More than 50,000 copies of *Disciplines* are sold each year, making it a perennial bestseller by publishing standards.

OF THE PEOPLE, FOR THE PEOPLE

In the 1960s, The Upper Room, like the rest of the world, was changing. Dr. Potts was a forward-thinking man. Committed to equality for all persons (even before that stance was popular), he once again recognized the gifts of Mary Ruth Coffman and moved her from the radio department to become an editorial associate, the first woman to bear that title at The Upper Room. (Mary Ruth would go on to become senior editor of *alive now!* magazine, and, near the end of her thirty-eight years with the ministry, director of production for

all Upper Room publications—books as well as magazines.) Dr. Potts also appointed Clarice Winstead to be associate dean and then dean of The Upper Room Chapel. He hired the Reverend Maurice King, the first African American to serve on the staff. Reverend King later became dean of The Upper Room Chapel.

Dr. Potts also began a practice that still shapes each issue of *The Upper Room*. Believing that the magazine's strength grew from its appeal to all kinds of people, and that all staff members had wisdom to offer, he involved the entire staff in choosing which meditations to publish. With fewer than a dozen persons on staff, everyone could fit at the conference table. But "copy session," as these meetings came to be known, can no longer include all the editorial and program staff, since they now number more than thirty. So the model has been adapted to

The publication of an issue of a periodical does not just happen—yesterday it was not and today it is! Most of the meditations for *The Upper Room* come voluntarily or by generalized invitation. All meditations receive consideration, with the editor making final selections from recommended groupings.

From "copy session" where the meditations are chosen, to the mailing of The Upper Room in its finished form, people are involved.

Above, Mary Ruth Coffman and Dr. Ernest Arnold discuss tapings of family devotions.

At left top, in the 1960s, *The Upper Room* diversified its staff to be more inclusive. Editorial associates Chan-Hie Kim, Sulon Ferree, Mary Ruth Coffman, and Maurice King (extreme right) participate with editor Wilson Weldon and managing editor Russell Chilcote (second from right) in making final selection of meditations to be published in the magazine.

Dr. Wilson O. Weldon served as world editor from 1967 to 1976.

include a representative from each magazine, from book publishing, and from the program area. The group deliberates over each meditation being considered for an issue of *The Upper Room*. This way of working has become a practice in discernment that shapes and affects The Upper Room's work on other tasks as well—and it is rooted in Manning Potts's egalitarian practice and respect for those with whom he worked.

In 1967, after leading the ministry for almost twenty years, Dr. Potts retired to Florida. (Dr. Potts's friend and former traveling companion, Harry Denman, retired the next year.) Showing that all his years of promoting interdenominational friendship were more than just talk, in retirement Dr. Potts took a position as pastor of an interdenominational church. He served there until he died after a heart attack in 1973.

Manning Potts's successor as editor of *The Upper Room* was someone who had been involved in its ministry for more than 20 years—Wilson O. Weldon. As chapter 2 noted, Dr. Weldon wrote the meditation that appeared in the magazine on April 15, 1944—the day of the memorial service for its first editor, Grover Emmons. Dr. Weldon continued to lead the ministry in the spirit of Manning Potts, welcoming Martin Luther King Sr. to speak in chapel in 1968.

Close friends Maurice King and Tom Page, both talented musicians, entertain at a staff Christmas function.

An ad that appeared in *The Tennessean* on December 29, 1962.

That same year, the Methodist Church and the Evangelical United Brethren Church (EUB) merged to become The United Methodist Church. Also that year, the General Board of Evangelism brought onto the staff in Nashville a musical group called Dust and Ashes. The singers, Tom Page and Jim Moore, were two young, long-haired, songwriting clergy fresh out of seminary in Washington, DC. Their hiring showed that the leaders of The Upper Room were open to new approaches to ministry. Later, because of his theological training, Tom Page was hired by Dr. Weldon as an editorial associate. Tom helped edit *The Upper Room* magazine and worked with Upper Room Books to produce *The Upper Room Disciplines.* Tom would be the resident long-haired nonconformist at 1908 Grand Avenue for more than twenty years, continuing his music ministry as a sideline while working as an editor.

THE BEST DECADE YET

By the mid-1960s, The Upper Room's international publishing had grown so much that it required more time and energy than Dr. Potts could give. Dr. Potts brought onto the staff a retired Navy chaplain, R. W. Ricker, to serve as the first full-time worker with international editions. "Rick" continued and strengthened international partnerships, remaining on staff into the 1980s.

In this decade, circulation of English-language versions of *The Upper Room* magazine topped 3.25 million. Upper Room Books published resources that addressed the holy habits of prayer, Bible study, and service in the name of Christ. International partnerships were strong. As the 1960s drew to a close, the ministry was thriving.

From left, Dr. R. W. Ricker, Rev. Sun Chool Chough, Russell Chilcote, and Rev. Chan-Hie Kim discuss the symbolism of the Agape Garden and the sculpture of Jesus and the Samaritan woman at the well during a visit by the Korean clergy in 1968.

Decade Highlights

1960

The Upper Room "Christmas Is" Radio Series receives Freedoms Foundation at Valley Forge award.

1961

The Upper Room receives Associated Press award for Superior Achievement in Its Field.

1963

318 millionth copy of the magazine is printed.

Editions now total 41 in 35 languages.

Pocket Prayer Books reach a total of 2.3 million copies sold.

1967

416 millionth copy of *The Upper Room* is printed.

Editions total 45 in 38 languages.

Circulation of the magazine reaches an estimated 3 million copies, with an estimated 10 million readers around the world.

The meditations united people in reading the same passage of scripture and listening for God's message to them in the words of a Christian brother or sister who might live 10,000 miles away.

THE 1970S: People Embracing the World

Chapter 5

As the tumultuous 1960s became the 1970s, *The Upper Room* magazine was printed in 37 languages. Copies were mailed or carried into more than 50 countries around the world. In the United States, a one-year personal subscription cost $5.00.

In addition to publishing the magazine, The Upper Room continued its work of publishing devotional books. But change was on the horizon, in publishing and in programs to support prayer and other spiritual practices.

Slogans from the 1960s such as "Never trust anyone over 30" and "Question authority" reflected a new attitude in the country. News reports about "flower children," riots, and antiwar demonstrations on college campuses shone a spotlight on unhappy young adults. Concerned parents and pastors sought to draw them back into the church and into relationship with Christ.

The Upper Room chapel and museum continued to be a major tourist destination in Nashville.

Left, the original *alive now!* staff, left to right: Janice Grana, Maurice King, Mary Ruth Coffman, Ron Patterson, and Donna Seymour.

Below, the first volume of *alive now!* from 1971.

A NEW AGE DAWNING

In response to this concern, The Upper Room staff began exploring new approaches to devotional life. They called for something less structured than *The pper Room* daily guide with its weekly themes (it was "over 30," after all)—someing younger and edgier. Experimental. Interactive. Colorful. A young woman amed Janice Grana (remember this name) joined the staff as an editorial assoate and helped shape a new resource—the ministry's first new periodical in 35 ears. This magazine invited readers to consider art, poetry, fiction, personal ignettes, and other Christian writing in varied formats. In 1971 Ron Patterson ecame its founding editor. The title of the magazine, *alive now!* looked as if it ad been produced on a dot-matrix printer—reflecting the computer age that as emerging.

Changes within The United Methodist Church continued to influence and ape the ministries of The Upper Room. In 1972, several United Methodist boards ere combined to form the General Board of Discipleship. Housed partly with pper Room offices in the (renamed after Harry) Denman Building, the Genral Board of Discipleship's mandate—to strengthen the witness of laity—fit well with The Upper Room's work. From its beginning the magazine had helped people form the habits of daily Bible reading and personal prayer, the backbone of effective ministry. And Grover Emmons, Roy Short, Harry Denman, and Manning Potts had used the magazine as part of evangelism efforts; their international travels and contacts opened the door for creation of many of the editions outside the United States.

The radio ministry of the 1940s and 1950s with its vinyl records gave way in the 1970s to a cassette edition of *The Upper Room.* Shown here are Dr. Rhoda Edmiston, a former Christian educator, and Mary Ruth Coffman, producer of the cassette edition. For many years Mary Ruth was the female voice heard on the cassette edition.

FORTY YEARS OF REACHING OUT

By its fortieth anniversary in 1975, *The Upper Room* was printed in 40 languages and 49 editions. The "little" magazine nurtured a community of believers that stretched around the world. Each day's meditation united people in reading the same passage of scripture and listening for God's message to them in the words of a Christian brother or sister who might live 10,000 miles away. Back in 1935 the Board of Home Missions, Evangelism, and Hospitals had approved publication of one test issue of a daily devotional magazine as an experiment—and its amazing growth brought about unprecedented cooperation in publishing among Christians around the world.

Opposite, one of the highlights of the 1970s was a gathering of representatives of *The Upper Room* editions from around the world to celebrate the 40th anniversary of the magazine.

Dr. Wilson Weldon, world editor of *The Upper Room*, presents the first copy of *Saat Tedeh*, the Indonesian edition, to Esther Simandjuntak, a graduate student at Scarritt College and cousin of the Indonesian editor, Alfred Simandjuntak. On the right is Dr. R. W. Ricker, associate and foreign editor.

Many denominations in addition to The United Methodist Church used and distributed the magazine in the United States. In other countries, *The Upper Room* was approved and recommended by the United Church of Canada; The United Churches of Christ in Japan, the Philippines, and Thailand; the Methodist Churches of Australasia and of New Zealand; the Armenian Evangelical Christian Endeavor Union of Syria and Lebanon; the West Pakistan Christian Council; the Andhra Christian Council in India; the Voice of the Gospel (Greek publishers); the Christian Lay Movement and Christian Literature Society in Korea; the Federal Council of the Churches of Italy; the Evangelical Confederation of Brazil—and others.

To mark the magazine's anniversary and this amazing publishing feat, delegates from 36 international editions were invited to Nashville, Tennessee. The historic gathering was both a celebration and a training event. International partners learned from a translation expert and from presentations about printing processes, business operations, and promotion to benefit their magazines. In coming to Nashville, many of the edition representatives journeyed outside their home country for the first time in their lives. With delight Upper Room staff met face-to-face friends they had corresponded with often, sometimes for

Maxie Dunnam became the new world editor in 1978. His *Workbook of Living Prayer* has sold over 250,000 copies since its publication in 1975.

years, in our common work of helping people learn to listen to God. Pictures taken during the event vividly illustrate the worldwide reach of the magazine.

NEW REALITIES, NEW INITIATIVES

Facing another reality of churches in the United States—an aging population—The Upper Room listened again and, in 1974, launched a large-print edition of *The Upper Room*. With very little promotion, its circulation climbed quickly and steadily. By the end of the decade, the large-print magazine often sold out its almost 100,000 copies of each issue.

The success of *The Upper Room* magazine made it possible to expand the work into other ministries. In response to the continuing call to strengthen Christian family life and help parents rear children in the faith, The Upper Room added a staff position called Director of Family Devotional Life. Constituents also

The "Alone with God" prayer room, adjacent to The Upper Room Chapel, is dedicated to the memory of Grover C. Emmons. It accommodates 8 people.

continued to ask for prayer and for help in learning to pray. To answer this call and allow more deliberate ministry, Wilson Weldon created the position of Director of Prayer Life and Fellowship and recruited a clergyman from California—Maxie Dunnam—to fill it. Maxie (another name to remember) came to The Upper Room with a passion for prayer and for using every available means to reach and teach people. Looking to the then-new technology of videocassette recorders, the year after he joined the staff, Maxie led in creating a series of videos on prayer. One of these featured Metropolitan Anthony Bloom, a leader in the Russian Orthodox Church, showing once again the continued ecumenical commitment and international reach of this ministry.

The heart of the Prayer Fellowship work was a daily period of prayer, observed in the prayer room in cooperation with the chapel hostess.

HELPING PEOPLE PRAY

The Prayer Fellowship was not so much a new ministry as a maturing of the organization's long-standing practice. Letters written by staff as far back as the 1930s refer often to prayer requests and staff meetings in which readers and their requests

Mrs. John M. Cate, senior hostess of The Upper Room, explains the symbolism of the World Christian Fellowship Window to Terri Lynn Hardin and her brother, Ray Dean Hardin, in 1970. Mrs. Cate greeted more than 500,000 visitors to The Upper Room Chapel during her tenure from 1958 to 1970.

were brought before God. This ministry grew as the numbers of readers increased, and beginning in 1949, Upper Room Fellowship staff corresponded with readers who asked for prayer and with people who needed the magazine but could not pay for it. They also responded to requests from military chaplains for copies of the magazine to give to service personnel, continuing a practice that began during World War II. But Maxie Dunnam led in organizing and deepening the ministry of praying for constituents and added a new ministry of teaching about prayer.

Mrs. Robert E. Christmas and daughter, Edna Earle, look on as Dr. Wilson O. Weldon presents a certificate to Mr. Robert E. Christmas (second from left), the one millionth visitor to The Upper Room Chapel.

The first new effort, the Adventure in Living Prayer retreat, was developed and used in churches throughout the United States. Trained leaders presented the two-day model, and a network of praying churches began to form naturally. The popularity of this model for group learning called forth resources to be used in groups—and signaled what would become a major new emphasis in the work of The Upper Room. Maxie Dunnam wrote a group study guide that taught the basics of prayer. The immediate success of *The Work-*

book of Living Prayer, published in 1975, demonstrated people's willingness and eagerness to learn how to pray. *The Workbook of Intercessory Prayer* soon followed. Who would have expected *The Workbook of Living Prayer* to stay in print for decades? Yet by the time a revised edition was published to celebrate its twentieth anniversary, more than a quarter of a million copies of this workbook were in the hands of praying people. This strong and sustained response proved that people want to pray and connect with God; they just need help getting started and support to keep on praying.

The Upper Room Living Prayer Center, created in 1977, expanded the prayer ministry. Operated by volunteers trained by Upper Room staff, the Prayer Center received prayer requests mailed in or called in on a toll-free telephone line and prayed for each person by name. Phone-forwarding technology made it possible to divert

The original and 20th anniversary editions of Maxie Dunnam's *Workbook of Living Prayer*

Excerpt from an article about The Upper Room Prayer Center in the *Arizona Daily Sun*, October 2002. Used by permission.

Don't have a prayer? Prayer lines mean you can always call for one

Mary O. Benedict, manager of the Upper Room prayer line, said callers like the anonymity the ministry offers. Volunteers ask only for first names and home state or country, but providing even that information is optional.

The telephone requests are forwarded around the world to 350 prayer groups who recite the prayer for 30 days.

calls to trained volunteers in their homes. Over the next few years, hundreds of compassionate people volunteered to pray for those in need. Volunteers signed up for two-hour blocks of time, many for the same two hours each week, some serving faithfully for years. Churches around the country also used this technology to become remote prayer centers. Many still do this; some make ministry as a remote prayer center on Thanksgiving or Christmas a tradition for their congregation.

Establishing prayer groups extended the center's ministry even further. Groups whose members completed specific studies about prayer became chartered Upper Room prayer groups, with prayer requests relayed to them weekly from Nashville. Within a few years, chartered groups existed throughout the United States and in Mexico.

On the wall of the Living Prayer Center, a large map of the United States dotted with colored pushpins designated locations of these prayer groups,

Below: The Upper Room Living Prayer Center opened in April 1977. Evelyn McKee was hired as the Prayer Center coordinator in 1979. She served faithfully in this position until her retirement in 1992.

Right: In March 1982, the Prayer Center hours expanded around the clock, and Betty Stroud was hired as night assistant. She was affectionately referred to as Sister Night Eagle. Betty worked the night shift until her retirement in 2009.

with large clusters of pins in some areas. Once when my daughter was about five, she asked what the pins meant. I told her that each one represented a group of people who get together to pray for people who call or write us asking for prayer. She pointed to an area in the western United States with very few pins over a large area and asked if that meant we had no prayer groups there. When I said yes, she asked, "What are we going to do about that?" What The Upper Room did, of course, was to continue to charter prayer groups and ask people to help us pray for those in need. At this time the Prayer Center received as many as 3,000 prayer requests per week.

The Upper Room staff in the mid-1970s. Front row (L to R): Janice Grana, Wilson O. Weldon, Cindy McGarry, Sulon Ferree, Chan Hi Kim, Lois Pottle, Bill English. Back row: Maxie Dunnam, Jo Kimmel, Brooks Little, R. W. Ricker, Mary Hall, Mary Ruth Coffman, Maurice King, Tom Page.

PRAYER IN ACTION

The year after the launch of the Living Prayer Center, Wilson Weldon retired as editor of *The Upper Room* magazine. His successor was someone already familiar with and enthusiastic about the work of The Upper Room—Maxie Dunnam.

Mary Ruth Coffman in the Agape Garden

Soon after becoming editor, Dr. Dunnam led the organization into learning about and adopting the Roman Catholic Cursillo (Spanish for "short course") model for training in Christian spirituality and service. The three-day Cursillo retreat helps participants understand God's grace more fully and inspires them to embody God's grace in their congregation. Several staff members, including Mary Ruth Coffman (then editor of *alive now!*) and Danny Morris (who had come on staff as Director of Prayer Life and Fellowship when Dr. Dunnam became editor) were scouts in this new endeavor. These staff members attended a Roman Catholic Cursillo in Peoria, Illinois, to see whether The Upper Room might adopt and adapt the model. In 1978, the first Upper Room Cursillo was held in Nashville. As with all Upper Room programs, the Cursillo was open to people of all denominations, and teams included people from many Christian traditions. Within a few years, The Upper Room Cursillo became The Walk to Emmaus, drawing its name from the Bible story recounted in Luke 24:13-35. Successive Emmaus weekends created a community of "pilgrims" who had "made their walk." Soon the Nashville group invited people from other cities and states to participate in weekends here, and The Walk to Emmaus became a movement that spread first to other states and then to other countries. By

1988, Emmaus communities existed in 60 countries. Over the last 30 years, thousands of pilgrims around the world have continued to be blessed by this ministry. In 2008 there were 393 Emmaus communities in 38 countries. Resources for The Walk to Emmaus were being published in 14 languages. The newest Emmaus community at the time of this writing is in Satka, Russia.

As the power of small groups, retreats, and other contemplative practices became evident, The Upper Room began to explore and develop new models that shaped the ministry in the next decade.

The Upper Room is still about people, thousands of people around the world who pray for and learn from one another through our magazines and through Upper Room programs such as The Walk to Emmaus.

Decade Highlights

1974

Large-print edition of *The Upper Room* is launched.

1975

The Workbook of Living Prayer is published.

1977

The Upper Room Living Prayer Center is established.

1978

First Upper Room Cursillo is held (later renamed The Walk to Emmaus).

The 1980s

brought many new milestones and new people who launched and shaped emerging ministries.

The 1980s: People Willing to Risk

Chapter 6

In 1980, the 600 millionth copy of *The Upper Room* came off the press. That figure is not a typo. *Six hundred million* copies of the small devotional guide had been published in English alone. That 600 million does not include circulation in other languages and countries—39 languages as the decade began.

The 1980s brought many other milestones and new people who launched and shaped emerging ministries. The first of these new ventures came about because of repeated requests from readers. Over five decades, *The Upper Room* magazine had served adults and families; our book publishing and retreat programs had enriched the prayer and devotional life of many adults. But as the new decade began, more and more constituents asked for a children's magazine. At The Upper Room we believe that God speaks to us through one another; every day the personal witnesses of faith that make up *The Upper Room* magazine illustrate our commitment to that truth.

This truth also shapes our pattern for developing new ministries. So, building on what we were hearing from our readers and from people in churches,

Rueben Job served as world editor from 1982 to 1984. His tenure as world editor was cut short when he was elected as a bishop in The United Methodist Church.

Debbie Keller, assistant marketing director; Carolyn Simms, assistant to the director of production; Sally McCanner, marketing assistant; and Beth Richardson, assistant editor for *Alive Now*, enjoy a staff break. Debbie went on to become director of production, Sally became associate director of production, and Beth became director of electronic publishing.

we pulled together a team—Christian educators, local-church leaders who worked with children, parents, and some people who were simply excited about the idea of a children's magazine.

This team began to dream. How might we lead children into a deeper life with God? Could a children's magazine be financially feasible? Would such a magazine fit with our mission? A magazine for children would have to be printed in color to appeal to them, and color printing costs a lot. Could we risk it? The Upper Room is not subsidized by any church or organization; it operates entirely on what we earn from selling what we publish, and on gifts from those who care about what we do and want to be part of it. Income from sales of magazines provides money to print upcoming ones. Even with extensive figuring and planning, the decision to move ahead would be a leap of faith. We adopted what has come to be our model in creating new products: listen, pray, talk, research, pray, wait, talk some more, wait, pray some more—and, finally, decide together. This consensus approach reflects and grows from the way we choose what we publish in *The Upper Room* magazine.

After much prayer and with encouragement from our constituents, we committed to creating the magazine. First, we searched for an editor. After several

The Reverend Judy Smith joined The Upper Room staff in 1981 to develop *Pockets*, our magazine for children. Shown below is the founding staff of *Pockets*: Kerry Blackwood, Judy Smith, and Janet McNish.

At left, a precocious cat named Bobo reads the first issue of *Pockets.*

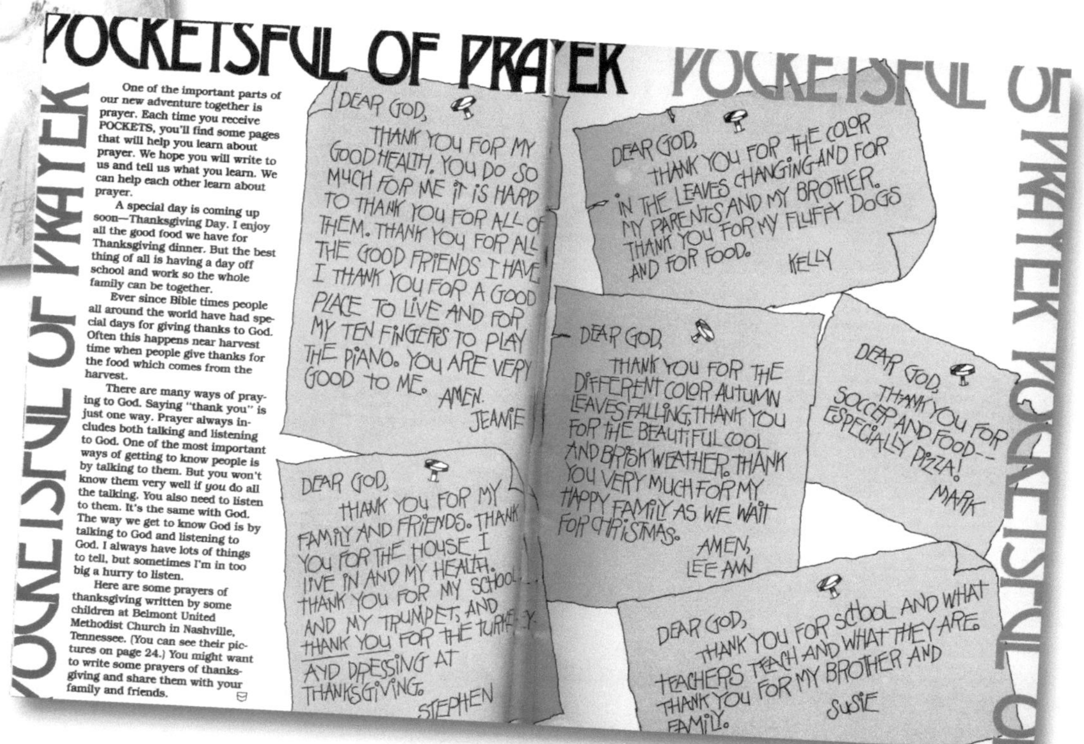

POCKETSFUL OF PRAYER

One of the important parts of our new adventure together is prayer. Each time you receive POCKETS, you'll find some pages that will help you learn about prayer. We hope you will write to us and tell us what you learn. We can help each other learn about prayer.

A special day is coming up soon—Thanksgiving Day. I enjoy all the good food we have for Thanksgiving dinner. But the best thing of all is having a day off school and work so the whole family can be together.

Ever since Bible times people all around the world have had special days for giving thanks to God. Often this happens near harvest time when people give thanks for the food which comes from the harvest.

There are many ways of praying to God. Saying "thank you" is just one way. Prayer always includes both talking and listening to God. One of the most important ways of getting to know people is by talking to them. But you won't know them very well if *you* do all the talking. You also need to listen to them. It's the same with God. The way we get to know God is by talking to God and listening to God. I always have lots of things to tell, but sometimes I'm in too big a hurry to listen.

Here are some prayers of thanksgiving written by some children at Belmont United Methodist Church in Nashville, Tennessee. (You can see their pictures on page 24.) You might want to write some prayers of thanksgiving and share them with your family and friends.

DEAR GOD, THANK YOU FOR MY GOOD HEALTH. YOU DO SO MUCH FOR ME IT IS HARD TO THANK YOU FOR ALL OF THEM. THANK YOU FOR ALL THE GOOD FRIENDS I HAVE. I THANK YOU FOR A GOOD PLACE TO LIVE AND FOR MY TEN FINGERS TO PLAY THE PIANO. YOU ARE VERY GOOD TO ME. AMEN. JEANIE

DEAR GOD, THANK YOU FOR THE COLOR IN THE LEAVES CHANGING AND FOR MY PARENTS AND MY BROTHER. THANK YOU FOR MY FLUFFY DOGS AND FOR FOOD. KELLY

DEAR GOD, THANK YOU FOR MY FAMILY AND FRIENDS. THANK YOU FOR THE HOUSE I LIVE IN AND MY HEALTH. THANK YOU FOR MY SCHOOL AND MY TRUMPET, AND THANK YOU FOR THE TURKEY AND DRESSING AT THANKSGIVING. STEPHEN

DEAR GOD, THANK YOU FOR THE DIFFERENT COLOR AUTUMN LEAVES FALLING, THANK YOU FOR THE BEAUTIFUL COOL AND BRISK WEATHER. THANK YOU VERY MUCH FOR MY HAPPY FAMILY AS WE WAIT FOR CHRISTMAS. AMEN, LEE ANN

DEAR GOD, THANK YOU FOR SOCCER AND FOOD-- ESPECIALLY PIZZA! MARK

DEAR GOD, THANK YOU FOR SCHOOL AND WHAT TEACHERS TEACH AND WHAT THEY ARE. THANK YOU FOR MY BROTHER AND FAMILY. SUSIE

months, the Reverend Judy Smith accepted the position. She moved with her family across the country, not knowing whether the magazine would succeed. When asked why she made that leap of faith, she said, "Because I sensed God calling me here." Many Upper Room staff persons answer the same way when asked why they work with this ministry.

Once we came up with a plan for the magazine, we held a contest among staff to come up with a name. The new magazine would be called *Pockets*. The winning suggestion came from Bob Wood, leader of The Walk to Emmaus program and father of three. Children responded well to the test issue, and regular publication began in 1981.

Other ministries also grew. In 1983, the Living Prayer Center received 9,000 calls per month from people requesting prayer. There were 25 Walk to Emmaus communities (local groups that sponsor Emmaus weekends) in the United States. The warm response to other Upper Room retreats proved that people appreciated a contemplative approach to spiritual growth. Danny Morris, director of The Upper Room Living Prayer Center, began to explore contemplative spirituality. He came up with an idea for something completely new: an intensive program to teach the history and classic practices of Christian spirituality to people as they experienced contemplative community. A group was assembled to, as Danny put it, "better up" his idea. Leaders from many different spiritual traditions, faculty from various programs in spirituality, and scholars gathered to refine the proposal.

In 1983, after five years of preparation, The Upper Room launched the two-year Academy for Spiritual Formation at the Scarritt-Bennett Center in Nashville, Tennessee. With leadership and participants from various Christian traditions, this first Academy offered a unique experience in spiritual community by providing times of worship, silence, lectures, and small groups. Twenty-seven two-year academies have been completed since 1983, with more than 1,200 graduates from 37 denominations. The daily rhythm of The Academy, with morning prayer, Holy Communion, and night prayer, provides a balance of head and heart, academic and practical wisdom. Meeting quarterly for five-day sessions over a period of two years, participants learn in-depth when they are together and then return to their homes

Danny Morris, whose dream became The Academy for Spiritual Formation, served on The Upper Room staff for more than twenty years.

The Upper Room

Right: This Academy for Spiritual Formation logo ties in with 2 Kings chapter 2, in which the mantle of God's Spirit passes from Elijah to Elisha. In the same way, the Academy seeks to pass on the mantle of the Spirit to each participant.

to live out what they have learned. Two-year academies have been held in Tennessee, Indiana, Alabama, California, Wisconsin, Texas, and Maryland.

An adaptation of this model, The Five-Day Academy for Spiritual Formation, began in 1985 in Mitchell, South Dakota. Locally sponsored, this one-time experience in Christian community has been offered in 43 states, using the same daily rhythm of worship, contemplation, lecture, and small-group learning as the two-year academy. About ten Five-Day Academies are held each year.

Just as The Academy began, Dr. Dunnam announced that he was leaving The Upper Room. The person chosen to succeed him as world editor, Dr. Rueben Job, was not new to the organization. In 1968 Dr. Job had been named to lead Tidings (which became Discipleship Resources), the publishing unit for the Board of Evangelism. Later Dr. Job served as associate general secretary of the Board of Discipleship, the successor to the Board of Evangelism. Dr. Job's leadership style was as quiet and gentle as Maxie Dunnam's had been outspoken and flamboyant—and just as effective. Rueben's patient, contemplative approach to everything he did steadied the burgeoning organization.

The Walk to Emmaus program was growing like a teenager—so fast that at times it was almost more than we could keep up with. Manuals for leaders helped

Opposite page: The Academy for Spiritual Formation has trained leaders from more than 30 denominations in contemplative practices and the history of Christian spirituality. The photo shows participants in Academy #1, held in Nashville in May 1983. **Row 1:** Janice Grana, Trudy Barlow, Betty Fribance, Jeanne Varnelle, Katherine DeGrow, Judith Barr, Theo Amenda, Bobbie Pratt. **Row 2:** Steve Bryant, John Spillman, John Miller, W. G. Henry, Claude Whitehead, Elise Eslinger, Sandy Fanning, Peggy Scott, Troy Ann Earle, Marie Roy, Bob Dungy, Tom Hawkins, Bruce Ough, Jan Caruso, Janet McCue, Barbara Wendland. **Row 3:** Judy Kerr, Bob Paul, Charles Gipson, David Moore, Miki Garrison, Peter Moore-Kochlacs, John Carmody, Bob Wood. **Row 4:** Charles Lee, Jim Perdue, Kathy Trotter, Jim Koob, Don Lefelar, Harry Beardsley, Eugene Blair, Bert Goodwin, Kent Millard, Danny Morris, Stewart Jackson, Rueben Job, Doug Anderson. **Row 5:** Frank Padgett, Charles Alexander, Henry Masters, Eldon Harzman, Norris Keirn, John Freer, John Mogabgab, Berkeley Poole, Adrian Cole, Mac Smith, Bob Mulholland.

Above: The Walk to Emmaus became an international movement in 1984. **Right:** Chrysalis, the youth and college-age counterpart to The Walk to Emmaus, also began in 1984. **Below:** Bob Wood, the first director of The Walk to Emmaus, is shown here with Betty Sue Moore, his assistant.

communities remain faithful to The Upper Room model as thousands of people "made their walk." These "pilgrims" returned to their home churches ready to serve Christ in new and deeper ways. In 1984 this interdenominational movement (and it was indeed a movement rather than just a program) became international with the first Walk to Emmaus in Australia. Chrysalis, a youth and college-age counterpart of The Walk to Emmaus, also launched that year.

Soon after Dr. Job became world editor, we began exploring the possibility of a new magazine to support Christian leaders in search of a deeper life in the Spirit. The idea for this resource had emerged during meetings to create The Academy for Spiritual Formation.

In the midst of this work, Dr. Job was elected a bishop. This came as a surprise to our staff. He was a delegate to United Methodists' 1984 meeting of the North Central Jurisdiction, the gathering that elects the church's bishops. Dr. Job was not in the initial group of candidates for bishop, but voting became deadlocked. In a rare move, someone nominated him from the floor as a new candidate—and soon he was elected. We rejoiced for The United Methodist Church and applauded the delegates' wisdom, but Dr. Job's election meant he would leave us to assume episcopal duties just two months later.

In the mid-1980s, The Walk to Emmaus movement traveled to reach those inside prison walls, with retreats being held at prisons in many locations. Pictured here are the team and pilgrims from a 1986 Walk at the Tennessee State Prison for Women.

Facing this unexpected and sudden change unsettled staff members. But the search committee for a new world editor found an able candidate already on staff: Janice Grana. She had come to The Upper Room as an editorial associate in 1971. Then she moved to a book-editor position. During Maxie Dunnam's time as our leader, she became director of publishing and associate world editor, overseeing book and magazine publishing. Under the leadership of Dr. Ezra Earl Jones, executive of the General Board of Discipleship, Janice was the first woman to be named world editor. This choice delighted staff members.

Because Janice already knew the organization, ongoing projects continued with minimal disruption—including investigating the possibility of a new

'Upper Room' Started As Light in Dark Times

By RAY WADDLE
Tennessean Religion News Editor

What began as an idea to publish a spiritual guide for people in the dark times of the Great Depression has become a bi-monthly magazine read by 8 million people in 43 languages.

But in the 50 years of its existence, *The Upper Room*, a daily devotional guide published here by the United Methodist Church, has not changed its philosophy, according to its world editor, Janice Grana.

"It's still a devotional magazine designed to help people find God," she said this week.

About 700 people are expected to attend *The Upper Room*'s 50th anniversary dinner program Thursday at the Hyatt Regency ballroom. The keynote speaker will be Tilden Edwards, executive director of the Shalem Institute for Spiritual Formation in Washington, D.C.

The magazine provides a short meditation for each day of the year. A key to its success has been its common touch, suggested Grana, who became world editor last year. The meditations are written by "ordinary people" from all over the world, not professional writers, she said.

"The writers are our readers. The meditations are honest, simple, personable — ordinary people who express what it means to be faithful and find nourishment from God in the modern world," she said.

Each year, the editors receive up to 3,000 unsolicited meditations that compete for the 365 slots available. The honor of getting a meditation published in a magazine read by 8 million people worldwide usually outweighs the $10 that *The Upper Room* pays for each meditation used, she said.

Sales to local churches and other religious institutions account for 90% of the circulation, she said. About half of its readers are affiliated with denominations other than United Methodist.

Grana said the magazine's goal now is to broaden its outreach into countries that are short on Christian literature, especially in Africa.

The magazine has always been published in Nashville, ever since a group of women from a Methodist church in San Antonio, Tex., suggested the idea for a devotional guide to bring comfort to families struggling in the Depression, she said. The first edition sold 100,000 copies.

The magazine is part of the publishing and programming organization called Upper Room, operated by the United Methodist denomination and located at 1908 Grand Ave. Upper Room publishes three other magazines and about 25 books a year and develops church programs. About 200,000 people annually visit the Upper Room chapel, Grana said.

Above: This column, written in honor of *The Upper Room*'s 50th anniversary, appeared in *The Tennessean* on February 23, 1985. Permission granted to reprint this article, © 1985 by *The Tennessean.*

Far right: Janice Timmons Grana, world editor from 1984 to 1997

resource for Christian leaders. People like those drawn to The Academy were asking for continuing nourishment and challenge. We envisioned a magazine that went beyond a how-to approach, that drew leaders into a spirituality that was grounded in a deep life of prayer and contemplative experience. Publishing for this specialized, relatively small audience would bring special financial challenges. And the idea of a Protestant contemplative journal was something completely new.

But, following The Upper Room's model of much deliberation and prayer, we decided to move forward with the magazine by naming an editor. The ecumenical advisory group that created The Academy for Spiritual Formation had included a close associate of Father Henri Nouwen (a professor at Yale Divinity School who became a renowned spiritual

The 50th anniversary celebration of The Upper Room in 1985 presented an opportunity to gather together five world editors: Roy Short, Rueben Job, Wilson Weldon, Janice Grana, and Maxie Dunnam.

VOLUME 1, NUMBER 1 SEPTEMBER/OCTOBER 1986

Weavings
"Woven together in love"
A Journal of the Christian Spiritual Life

"A Serious Call to a Devout & Holy Life"

writer)—John Mogabgab. A man of deep faith, a theologian, and a gifted writer, John seemed a logical choice to shape the new magazine.

John came to The Upper Room as did leaders of our other new ventures—in a leap of faith, with no guarantees that the magazine would succeed or that he would have a job a year later. John assembled a team that outlined what this contemplative magazine should be: welcoming and thought-provoking, drawing on deep wisdom from many spiritual traditions but also reflecting emerging perspectives, an inviting experience for the eyes and the sense of touch as well as for the mind and heart. The theme of the first issue identified the desire we sought to address: "A Serious Call to a Devout and Holy Life." *Weavings: A Journal of the Christian*

Right, the founding staff of *Weavings*: Lynn Gilliam, associate editor; John Mogabgab, editor; and Peggy Moon, editorial assistant.

Spiritual Life premiered in September 1986. Like our other publications, *Weavings* reached across denominational lines from its first issue.

The Upper Room daily devotional guide also continued its reach into other countries. By the end of the decade, 62 editions in 42 languages were going into more than 80 countries. The vision of those who wanted to provide daily encouragement to people in their own languages drew us into publishing partnerships in Europe, Asia, and Africa. This decade of growth culminated in partnerships that would propel new programs in the 1990s.

Decade Highlights

1980

600 millionth copy of *The Upper Room* is printed.

1981

Pockets magazine is launched.

1982

Maxie Dunnam resigns; Rueben Job becomes world editor.

1983

First two-year Academy for Spiritual Formation is held.

1984

Rueben Job is elected bishop.

Janice Grana becomes first woman world editor.

Chrysalis is launched.

The Walk to Emmaus goes international.

1985

First Five-Day Academy for Spiritual Formation is held.

1986

Weavings journal begins publication.

The Upper Room

Website allows
people to contact us
continually and immediately,
in a variety of ways.

THE 1990S: People Taming Technology

Chapter 7

Though wonderful, growth is also sometimes painful. We found this to be true in new ways in the 1990s. Emerging technology and changing reader expectations combined to force changes in the ways we did our work.

In 1979, *The Upper Room* magazine's content—the meditations that make up each issue—was first typed on a typewriter and retyped after each round of editing. In 1980, we began using a magnetic-tape system that allowed us to type the content once and then make small alterations without retyping everything. Over the next few years, we used a variety of electronic systems as technology changed, moving to desktop computers in the early 1990s. The multiple, rapid changes we saw in our editorial processes mirrored the speed of changes in the technology used to handle subscriptions and mailings.

THE UPPER ROOM® DAILY DEVOTIONAL GUIDE

DEMANDS AND CHALLENGES

Since its launch in 1935, *The Upper Room* has been sold primarily to churches; the churches then distribute copies to their members. But through the 1970s and

Charlene Eubank, director of subscription services for *The Upper Room*, works with CDS in Boone, Iowa, to maintain subscriptions to all of our magazines. Charlene came to the General Board of Discipleship in 1968 and has served in a variety of roles at The Upper Room.

1980s, as people moved around the country and between churches, the numbers of our individual subscribers grew. By 1990, half a million people subscribed to our four magazines. In order to serve these readers well and get their magazines to them on time, we needed to manage mailings of literally millions of magazines and maintain records with hundreds of thousands of names and addresses.

The increasingly automated U.S. postal system also placed demands on how addresses and mailings were handled. The technology required us to operate efficiently, because mailing millions of magazines was phenomenally expensive. Operating the computer systems and software needed would require continual upgrading and highly trained staff.

So, in order to meet the standards that our readers set and to work efficiently, The Upper Room hired an outside company to maintain our subscriber records. But a team of people—many of whom had worked on the third floor at 1908 Grand Avenue for years—had been maintaining our records. With this outsourcing, we would no longer have jobs for all of them. For the first time in our history, we had to reduce staff, a step that was extremely painful. We were victims of our own success; there were more people wanting our magazines than our staff had the capacity to serve. And so we were forced to change.

NEW FORMATS, NEW OPPORTUNITIES

Facing the realities of technological change also led us to consider a computer edition of *The Upper Room*. Our first idea was to provide a version on floppy disk, but technology changed more quickly than we could plan and test such a product. The emerging Internet seemed the way of the future, so in the mid-1990s we created a position for a Web communicator. Beth Richardson, who had joined the staff as assistant editor of *Alive Now* magazine in 1986, moved into this role, becoming our self-described technogeek. Her creativity and skill guided the development of The Upper Room's Web site: www.upperroom.org. The site went live in 1996. Since then, upperroom.org has expanded greatly, winning numerous awards from religious communicators.

Our Web site allows people to contact us continually in a variety of ways. Prospective writers can go to

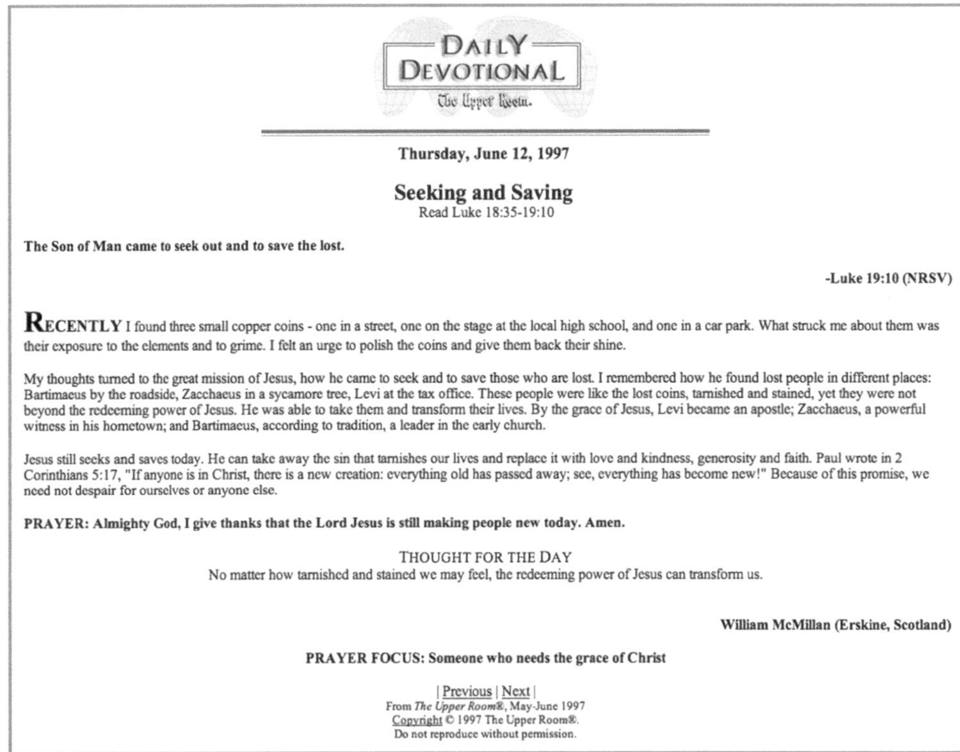

DAILY DEVOTIONAL
The Upper Room.

Thursday, June 12, 1997

Seeking and Saving
Read Luke 18:35-19:10

The Son of Man came to seek out and to save the lost.

-Luke 19:10 (NRSV)

RECENTLY I found three small copper coins - one in a street, one on the stage at the local high school, and one in a car park. What struck me about them was their exposure to the elements and to grime. I felt an urge to polish the coins and give them back their shine.

My thoughts turned to the great mission of Jesus, how he came to seek and to save those who are lost. I remembered how he found lost people in different places: Bartimaeus by the roadside, Zacchaeus in a sycamore tree, Levi at the tax office. These people were like the lost coins, tarnished and stained, yet they were not beyond the redeeming power of Jesus. He was able to take them and transform their lives. By the grace of Jesus, Levi became an apostle; Zacchaeus, a powerful witness in his hometown; and Bartimaeus, according to tradition, a leader in the early church.

Jesus still seeks and saves today. He can take away the sin that tarnishes our lives and replace it with love and kindness, generosity and faith. Paul wrote in 2 Corinthians 5:17, "If anyone is in Christ, there is a new creation: everything old has passed away; see, everything has become new!" Because of this promise, we need not despair for ourselves or anyone else.

PRAYER: Almighty God, I give thanks that the Lord Jesus is still making people new today. Amen.

THOUGHT FOR THE DAY
No matter how tarnished and stained we may feel, the redeeming power of Jesus can transform us.

William McMillan (Erskine, Scotland)

PRAYER FOCUS: Someone who needs the grace of Christ

| Previous | Next |
From *The Upper Room®*, May-June 1997
Copyright © 1997 The Upper Room®.
Do not reproduce without permission.

The Upper Room Web site went live in 1996. **Above:** A screen shot of the online meditation for June 12, 1997. **At left:** Beth Richardson continues to guide our electronic publishing.

Jerry Haas became the director for The Academy for Spiritual Formation in 1999.

our Web site and submit a meditation to be considered for publication in *The Upper Room*. A form on the site allows writers to submit contributions directly to our editorial offices. Writer's guidelines for Upper Room books and magazines can be accessed through the Web site, and themes for upcoming issues of our magazines appear on each magazine's pages within the Web site. The site also contains excerpts from many of our magazines, allowing readers to sample their content. The *Pockets* Web site offers young readers content in addition to what appears in the magazine; it gives their parents information about family devotional practices and children's spiritual development. Teens can visit *Devozine* magazine's site to connect with other readers and writers for that magazine and to interact with staff.

Danny Morris and Jerry Haas, the first and second directors of The Academy for Spiritual Formation

Visitors to the Web site can also read excerpts from Upper Room books and order books through the online bookstore. Each program of The Upper Room has its own area too. For example, Emmaus pilgrims anywhere in the world can visit the Emmaus site to find the community nearest them. Those interested in our international work can learn about magazine editions and programs outside the United States. Web visitors can leave requests for The Upper Room Living Prayer Center and messages for staff members.

In 1997, we launched online and e-mail versions of the daily devotional guide. At the time of this writing, 44,000 people receive the e-mail devotional each day, and about 12,000 people read the devotional on The Upper Room Web site. We are also planning to offer digital magazines. We've come a long way from the days of typewriters, word processors, and magnetic tape.

The electronic publishing staff takes time out for a little fun in the snow. Front row: Jane Massey, Beth Richardson, Sarah Parsons. Back row: Kathleen Stephens, Bill Treadway, Blanca Longhurst.

Sarah Schaller-Linn, international rights manager, and Lynne Deming, senior editor in Upper Room Books, "man" The Upper Room booth at the Frankfurt Book Fair in 2000.

GROWING OUR PUBLICATIONS

However, growth of our electronic presence and communication does not mean that traditional ink-and-paper publishing is no longer important. In the 1990s we continued to grow in that enterprise too. Part of Janice Grana's vision for our publishing was that it be an international exchange, not one-way, us-to-them. She wanted to reflect the witness of writers in other countries in our book publishing as we do in *The Upper Room* magazine. She also wanted our books with their excellent content to be translated for use by others. To this end, she appointed an international rights manager, Sarah Schaller-Linn, whose job included cultivating relationships with Christian publishers in other countries.

At the International Book Fair in Frankfurt, Germany, Sarah was invited to the first Shabbat service ever held at the Frankfurt Book Fair (as a guest of Jewish Lights Publishing) and to a dinner held by the Catholic Publishers Association. The ecumenical welcome she received shows that *The Upper Room* continues to be a bridge connecting people of different faith traditions through prayer and spirituality. Our display at the book fair included copies of *The Upper Room* in its many languages. People from around the world stopped to point out the version of the magazine that they read, illustrating the reach of our publishing. Manning Potts and Harry Denman's vision continues to be realized as prayer links God's people throughout the world.

Since 1996, numerous Upper Room titles have been translated into Korean and Portuguese; a number of Upper Room titles have been and continue to be available in Spanish. We have also copublished books with organizations in the United Kingdom. *Children and Prayer* by Betty Shannon Cloyd and *The Christ-Centered Woman* by Kimberly Dunnam Reisman have been especially welcomed in other countries. We continue to seek out publishers whose mission and vision fits with ours, in order to join them in publishing resources that make a difference in people's relationship with God and one another.

Some international editions of Upper Room books: *Children and Prayer*—UK edition; *El pastor como guía espiritual (The Pastor As Spiritual Guide)*—Spanish edition; *The Upper Room Disciplines 2001*—Chinese edition, 2006; *Quiet Spaces*—UK edition.

NEW MAGAZINES, NEW APPROACHES

Another international partnership, an unplanned one, became possible because of our magazine for teens, *Devozine*. *Devozine* launched in 1996, again because

may / june 1996

just for teens

Devo'Zine

Say-So's Kim Thomas: In-Between

Daily Prayer: Get Hitched!

What R U Searching 4?

New View of *Clueless*

Help! I NEED SPACE

Editor's note

Welcome to *Devo'Zine!*

This new devotional 'zine is just for you. As you read through this issue, you'll find lots of meditations and articles written by persons who are your age and by caring adults who work with youth.

The weekly themes in this first issue have to do with things we are seeking in life. I think we are all searching. We have questions. We have some answers. But we sure don't have it all figured out. In *Devo'Zine*, that's OK.

DZ is about real life.
DZ is written by real people.
DZ is about getting to know a real God.

In *Devo'Zine*, we'll be exploring together what it means to talk to God conversationally and to experience God's presence in scripture, in prayer, through other people, and in the middle of our everyday life in the world. I hope you'll think of Devo'Zine [illegible]

BELONGING@YOUR FINGERTIPS. YNOT? :-)

BRAD'S STORY:
A friend got me excited about using the computer to talk to other youth around the country. Since I already had a computer and a modem, I talked with my parents about signing up for an online service. After considering what this would mean, both financially and in terms of tying up our phone line, we decided to go for it. And I'm glad we did! I've discovered how important this online connection can be.

Recently, I moved from Virginia to Tennessee. About the same time, Cameron, a friend of mine, moved to Florida. Later, during a phone call to Bryan, an old friend from Virginia, we decided that our next "conversation" should be online—without long distance fees—and should include Cameron, since he subscribed to the same online service as we did. We met in a "private room" where all three of us were able to "talk" with each other. Being online has helped me to stay in touch with some really good friends!

RON'S STORY:
Being online has helped our youth group to stay in touch. This summer when Brad was at Bryan's house in Virginia, he would e-mail (electronic mail) me in Tennessee, and I would reply. John, another member of our youth group, spends summers in Florida with his grandparents. Using his cousin's online service, we were all able to keep up with one another for several months by way of computers. Members of our group took turns answering John's e-mail, so he heard from a variety of people and continued to be a part of the group while he was away.

E-mail the *Devo'Zine* staff (102615.3145@compuserve.com) and let us know your favorite places to talk to other youth online.

<< Brad McLaughlin and Ron Whitler >>

Places to be in touch (these will get you started):

Access	Key Word	Possibilities
America OnLine	Teen Scene	bulletin boards (social and spiritual issues), pen pals
CompuServe	Youth Drive! Forum (YDRIVE!)	weekly online teen conferences, discussion of life issues, creative options, media reviews
Internet	KIDLINK	global youth networking

12

NEXT DAY **Stretch**

Not everyone has access to e-mail or the Internet, but everyone has a need to belong. How do you stay in touch with persons who matter to you? How do you meet new friends? network with other youth? create community? Make a commitment to be more intentional about staying in touch. In fact, you know that call, letter, or visit you've been putting off? Do it today!

Brad McLaughlin (Darb78@aol. com)—a high school senior—and Ron Whitier (Frankyouth@aol com)—an adult youth worker at Brad's church in Franklin, Tennessee—delivered this article to Devo'Zine by electronic mail. :->

14 MAY/JUNE 1996

MAY/JUNE 1996 15

46

Devo'Zine Movie Review

Clueless

Heather S. Peck

Way popular, almost 16, very rich and quite "clued-in" to fashion, Cher (played by Alicia

SEARCHING IN THE DARK

continued →

MAY/JUNE 1996 49

Robin Pippin and Sandy Miller led a group that developed *Devo'Zine*, our magazine for teenagers.

of requests from our constituents. Parents, youth workers, and teens themselves wanted us to support young people with a devotional magazine designed specifically for them. As is our model, we assembled a team to investigate possibilities and create the magazine. We knew that teens would more willingly listen to one another than to adults, so *Devozine* is written by young people (mostly) for young people. Founding editor Robin Pippin led the team in creating a first issue that outraged some people with its wild design and bold colors. (We had expected this response.) Each issue of *Devozine* differs from the preceding one, continually changing to keep readers engaged.

The magazine circulated quickly to English-speaking countries outside the United States and opened the door to new ministry and new connections with readers and users. Soon after the launch of the magazine in 1996, Craig Mitchell, who works with youth in the Uniting Church in Australia, began writing guides for youth leaders to accompany each issue of the magazine. The guide offered suggestions for using the magazine in small groups. We heartily approved this mentor's guide and offered it within the United States to youth workers. When the church in Australia found the venture too expensive to continue, publication of the mentor's guide moved to Nashville. In January–February 1998, we

Here are recent issues of *Devozine*. Sandy Miller, **bottom right,** has been senior editor since 2003.

assumed printing and distribution of the *Guide for Mentors and Small Groups* to accompany each issue of *Devozine.* However, Craig and two collaborators, Cheryl Lawrie and Bruce Mullan, kept on writing the guide, sending it electronically to the *Devozine* staff to be printed. Our Australian friends wrote material for the guide for several years, in a productive partnership that taught us new ways of working and heralded what was to come.

Janice Grana, who led us through our tumultuous years of adapting to technology and entering cyberspace, retired from her position as world editor in 1997, after 26 years with The Upper Room. Her leadership, particularly in relation to international publishing, reflected the care we seek always to give to the global conversation among Christians.

NURTURING LEADERS

During the 1990s, support for spiritual leaders and for congregations emerged as another important emphasis for The Upper Room. Retired Bishop Rueben Job returned from Iowa to Nashville in 1992 with a vision of starting an international center for Christian spirituality. When Bishop Job retired again in 1995,

The Reverend Marjorie Thompson joined The Upper Room program staff in 1996 as director of the Pathways Center for Christian Spirituality, part of the Pathways Initiative.

a new vision called the Pathways Initiative began to form in the imagaination of Janice Grana and Stephen Bryant. It was comprised of three parts: the Pathways Center for Christian Spirituality, an outgrowth of Rueben's vision with an emphasis on programmatic events and resource development for congregational leaders; Pathways in Spiritual Growth, a publishing imprint specializing in book resources for the spiritual life of leaders; and the Pathways Network, an effort to connect leaders across the United States and denominations through a newsletter and Web site. Dr. Steve Harper led in launching the Pathways Network until his return to seminary education in 1998. Reverend Marjorie Thompson assumed leadership of the Pathways Center for Christian Spirituality, developing retreats to sustain the spiritual life of spiritual leaders guiding retreat leadership training, and crafting the structure of a new resource in small-group

Helen Burrus Photography

Stephen Bryant, director of Program Ministries, worked for a time on the team that developed *The Spiritual Formation Bible*. In 1997 he was named the eighth world editor of *The Upper Room*.

spiritual formation that became Companions in Christ.

The Upper Room's reputation as a leader in spiritual formation had been growing throughout the '80s and '90s. In 1997, Zondervan Publishers approached us to work with them to create *The Spiritual Formation Bible* "because The Upper Room knows about spiritual formation." They asked us to design the special additional features that would make this Bible a spiritual formation resource. We would be the "authors" of the project; Zondervan would print and distribute the Bible.

As always, we assembled an interdenominational team to work on the project. Dr. Timothy Jones, a graduate of Princeton Theological Seminary and an Episcopal clergyman, author, and editor, led the team. Stephen Bryant, director of Program Ministries at The Upper Room; JoAnn Miller, acquisitions editor for Upper Room Books; and I, Mary Lou Redding, completed the design group.

We dreamed up a Bible that offered "entry points" on every page to lead readers into *experiencing* the Bible, not just thinking about it. Writers of the entry points included Baptists, Episcopalians, Lutherans, Presbyterians, Quakers, members of the Reformed Church in America, United Methodists, Roman Catholics, and others. Later, *The Spiritual Formation Bible* would become *The Meeting God Bible*, published in 2009 by Upper Room Books. Some of this content and the Bible's spiritual formation approach also became the core of The Upper Room's "Meeting God in Scripture" series of six- and eight-week Bible studies for small groups.

Stephen Bryant was unable to continue working with the committee creating *The Spiritual Formation Bible*, however. He was chosen as Janice Grana's successor, becoming in July 1997 the eighth world editor of *The Upper Room*. Stephen would lead us into the new millennium and into new ministries.

Decade Highlights

1990

Growing subscriptions lead to outsourcing subscriber records.

1995

Pathways Center for International Spirituality is created.

1996

Devozine magazine for teens and mentor's guide for small groups is launched.

The Upper Room Web site goes live.

1997

Janice Grana retires; Stephen Bryant becomes world editor.

Online and e-mail editions of *The Upper Room* are launched.

1999

Jerry Haas becomes director of The Academy for Spiritual Formation.

The Upper Room and Zondervan partner to publish *The Spiritual Formation Bible*.

The worldwide community of prayer engendered by *The Upper Room* magazine continues to draw people together across oceans and continents.

THE NEW MILLENNIUM: People Welcoming the Digital Future

Chapter 8

The new millennium brought new milestones for The Upper Room. As the decade opened, *The Upper Room* magazine was published in 44 languages—more than ever before. In late 2009, the *one billionth* copy of *The Upper Room* will come off the press. That's *one thousand million copies.* Maybe as part of celebrating our seventy-fifth anniversary we should quit calling *The Upper Room* "that little magazine"! Its reach is huge, now going into more than 100 countries.

But wait—there's more! In 2001, we launched a Web site for young adults, MethodX.net (*Method* as in methodic or intentional, "X" from the well-known Christian symbol for the name *Christ*). Kathleen Stephens led in developing the format and content of our first completely nonprint publication. This Web site continues its outreach to young adults, though it is now sponsored by the Division on Ministries with Young People of the General Board of Discipleship.

Below: Kathleen Stephens, editor of MethodX.net, with an Upper Room staff group at Youth 2003. Also pictured are Sandy Miller, senior editor, *Devozine*; Bill Treadway, associate editor, MethodX; Brandon Dyce, marketing coordinator; and Nicole Corlew, associate editor, *Devozine*.

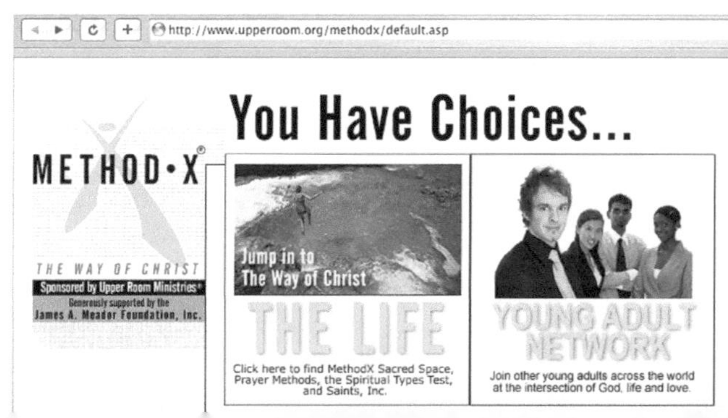

Left, Africa Upper Room Ministries staff (left to right) in 2008: Renny Stoltz, Bertina Mazibuko, Stephen D. Bryant (world editor, *The Upper Room*), Nancy Herron, Cheryl Pillay, Ike Moloabi, John Mitchley, Winifred Montgomery.

Right, Africa Upper Room Ministries staff members Nancy Herron, Ike Moloabi, John Mitchley, Renny Stoltz, and Ralph Willcox.

Above, Bishop Hans Växby reads his meditation at writer training in Estonia, November 2007.

Right, Bertina Mazibuko, Anathoth ground maintenance person, and Rev. Ike Moloabi.

Above, Beatrice Smith, editor of the Africa English edition, with her husband, Lindsay, who does all the prepress for the Portuguese and Africa English editions. They live in Cape Town.

Right, Clifton Harris and **below,** Dennis Stone record the audio version of *The Upper Room* in 2007.

A generous donor gave The Upper Room this house and some land in a small village outside Johannesburg, South Africa. In 2002 this building became the base of operations for the first international outpost of The Upper Room. Its name, Anathoth, echoes the prophet Jeremiah's symbolic act of trust in God.

WELCOMING NEW PARTNERS AND METHODS

In 2002, the year after the launch of MethodX.net, we embarked on another completely new venture: an international outpost. A generous donor gave us a house and a bit of land in a small village outside Johannesburg, South Africa, and Africa Upper Room Ministries (AURM) was born. We named the facility Anathoth, following the example of the prophet Jeremiah. (Jeremiah bought a parcel of land during the Babylonian Exile and named it Anathoth, which means hope, as a sign of trust in God to sustain God's people during their exile and as a reminder to God's people that they would someday return.) This new enterprise would shape The Upper Room's publications and programs.

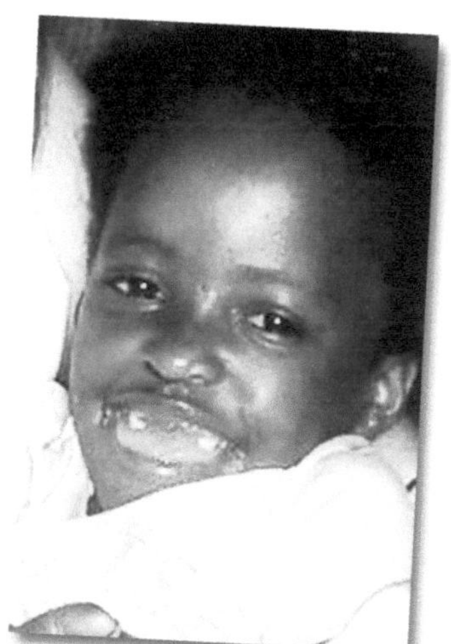

Left, Zanele Mazibuko came to live with her aunt on the Anathoth property. When they arrived, Zanele was ill from HIV infection, but after care from the people at Anathoth, she is doing well. Zanele is shown here (in the middle) with her cousins.

The Kiswahili edition of *The Upper Room* features African art.

A few years earlier, a South African man, Roland Rink, made his Walk to Emmaus in his home country. Roland returned from the Emmaus weekend with the beginning of a dream: that everyone on the continent of Africa would spend time with God every day. And this would be possible through their using *The Upper Room* magazine. Anathoth became the base for operations to help that dream come true. Soon after his Walk to Emmaus, Roland told us of his dream, and as had happened in earlier decades, Upper Room leaders listened to God's call in the vision of someone who came to us.

Roland Rink (managing director of Africa Upper Room Ministries), Philip Polo (editor of *The Upper Room* Kiswahili edition), and Dale Rust Waymack (Africa Region Coordinator—USA)

A short time later, Roland left his job with a telecommunications company and became the first employee of Africa Upper Room Ministries. He joined a line of others who made a leap of faith in order to work with The Upper Room. The South Africa

Mary Ann White ("Fellowship MAW"), left, visits with Evelyn McKee at a retirement reception.

English edition of *The Upper Room* was a first step. We hired additional African staff to adapt and add to the English edition to reflect and speak to their African situation.

Soon, Roy Govender, a South African man with a passion for small groups, came up with an idea: include discussion questions in each issue of *The Upper Room* to create an inexpensive small-group resource that anyone could easily use. Roy began writing them as his gift to the ministry. Each set of questions (one set per week) was unique, building on a meditation from that week. The questions and small-group meeting plan immediately became popular in South Africa. Learning from our African colleagues, we soon incorporated this feature into the U.S. English edition. The first set of discussion questions with a guide for weekly small-group meetings appeared in the May–June 2004 issue. This feature was an immediate hit. But we didn't know how big a hit until we omitted the small-group guide in the November–December 2004 issue to make room for an Advent study. Phone calls and e-mails of protest poured into our office in Nashville from groups that had been meeting weekly and wanted "their" questions. We quickly posted on our Web site small-group discussion questions to accompany the issue. Soon the Spanish edition of the magazine (*El Aposento Alto*) began including the

The Arabic and Africa Portuguese editions

small-group meeting guide and discussion questions. Then the Norwegian edition picked up the idea of posting the small-group content on the Internet—and so on. Ministry in Africa shaped our ministry and moved it in new ways to other countries and continents.

NEW EDITIONS, NEW MEDIA

Not everyone in Africa speaks and reads English. In 2001 *The Upper Room* was already being published in Arabic, French, Hausa, and Arabic. The Africa Portuguese edition began in 2002, using translated content from the Brazilian Portuguese edition. The dream of ministry throughout Africa included offering *The Upper Room* in at least six major languages: IsiZulu, IsiXhosa, Afrikaans, Sesotho, Setswana, and Africa English (contextualized English). The plan of our then-partners, The Methodist Church of South Africa, was to launch six new editions simultaneously or at least within the same year. We soon learned that we had to move more slowly, and we began to modify the plans and to experiment. The Africa French edition did not survive as a print product, but the radio broadcast of *The Upper Room* meditations in French reaches a wide audience. There are also daily broadcasts of the meditations in Kiswahili and IsiZulu, with plans to broadcast in Arabic in the near future. A book of 365 meditations translated from *The Upper Room* into Kiswahili was published in 2009.

Soon Africa Upper Room Ministries reached out to Christians in other African countries. After all, their dream is that everyone in Africa—the whole continent, not just the country of South Africa—will spend time with God every day. AURM began selling the magazine to other Afrian countries through distributors and in the process created much-needed jobs. AURM has partners in several countries, with distributors of the South Africa English edition of the magazine in Zimbabwe, Kenya, Mozambique, Swaziland, Botswana, Liberia, Côte d'Ivoire (Ivory Coast), and Lesotho. Anathoth also serves those living nearby as a base for worship, teaching, and feeding for young people in the area. In addition, mission groups will soon be housed there, moving out from the base to do their work. AURM plans to build a modest skills development center and to extend the book room and distribution center to accommodate the large demand for Upper Room resources.

These participants in an October 2008 writers conference in Nairobi are writing meditations for use in *The Upper Room* Africa edition.

Côte
D'Ivoire
Liberia
Kenya
Mozambique
Zimbabwe
Botswana
Lesotho
Swaziland
South
Africa

RESPONDING TO HURTING PEOPLE

One of the realities of life in South Africa and all over the African continent is AIDS. The HIV infection rate is extremely high. In some areas, health workers estimate that 60 percent of the populations they serve carry the virus. Africa Upper Room Ministries came to The Upper Room with another idea: create a small, inexpensive resource to offer comfort to those with HIV/AIDS and other serious illnesses. The resource would be modeled after *Prayers for Courage*, a resource created for military personnel; content would come from people living with HIV/AIDS, malaria, tuberculosis, and other serious illnesses. In 2007 The Upper Room created and jointly

United Methodist News Service photo by Kami L. Rice

Above, the Pocket Prayers series: *Prayers for Times of Illness; Prayers for Hope; Prayers for Courage* (published in 2003 for troops in the Iraq War); *Prayers for Encouragement* (published in 2007 for persons living with HIV and AIDS and other serious diseases); *Prayers for Hard Times* (published in 2009 for persons experiencing financial crisis). **Left,** street people in Cape Town, South Africa, hold copies of *Prayers of Encouragement*, a devotional booklet for people with HIV/AIDS and other serious illnesses. The booklets are provided through Africa Upper Room Ministries.

Above: An African adaptation of the Academy in Sedibeng, South Africa, in 2007. The leadership team included Vuyelwa Ntshinga, Ike Moloabi, Nwabisa Mabandla, Sidwell Mokgothu, Mogomotsi Diutlwileng, Jerry Haas, Roy Govender, and Greg Andrews. **Below:** Steve Byant enjoys playing drums with other Sedibeng participants.

published *Prayers for Encouragement*. Since then, this resource has been published in eleven languages. By summer 2008, over half a million copies of *Prayers for Encouragement* had been distributed.

AURM continued its reach beyond publishing. We also worked with church leaders to create Sedibeng, an African adaptation of The Academy for Spiritual Formation. Sedibeng modeled inclusiveness and reconciliation between formerly divided groups, deliberately seeking black, "coloured," and Caucasian participants. Now we are working with a group of leaders in India to adapt The Academy model for their culture as well.

Our model for international ministry was changing. Clearly, no one person could oversee all that was going on through our partnerships around the world. In 1998 Joan Floyd had joined the staff as coordinator of international ministries, handling all daily contacts with editors and translators via electronic communication and making onsite visits to strengthen relationships. World editor Steve Bryant invited other staff members to relate to our partners by region. Dale Rust Waymack had fallen in love with Africa and its people, so she took on responsibility for building relationships on the African continent. Tom Albin, dean of the chapel and team leader of program ministries, expressed interest in Asia and the Pacific Islands; Lynne Deming had a connection with Australia; Carmen Gaud, international editor of *El Aposento Alto*, would focus on Central and South America; I would relate to European editions; and Jerry Haas would develop relationships in India.

ON THE HOME FRONT

Our work in the United States also continues—and grows. The vision that has propelled us through the past several years is a vision of congregations as centers for spiritual formation. Our work with The Academy for Spiritual Formation and the various retreat models of The Upper Room show clearly the universal hunger to *experience*—not just read and learn about—God. Steve Bryant's dream to create a congregational resource to do this emerged in the 1990s; the dream became a reality in 2001 with the launch of *Companions in Christ*, a small-group resource. A phrase used to introduce the Companions series is "Expect to be transformed." People tell us that is what happens in their small groups.

Companions in Christ (CIC) is a 28-week journey to explore spiritual disciplines in Christian community. The five modules of CIC center on the

Companions in Christ is a congregational program and series of small-group resources to help people experience God's presence and learn to listen to God's voice.

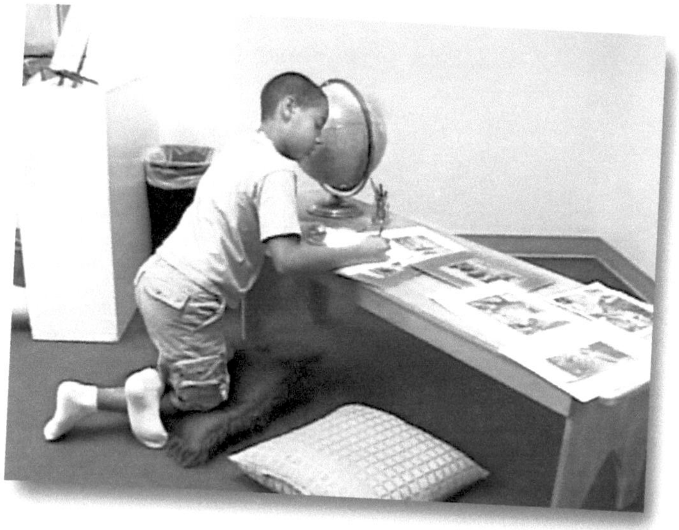

A child works at the Journaling reflection station in *The Way of the Child* at Lake Junaluska, North Carolina.

Christian life as a spiritual journey, scripture meditation, prayer, our call as followers of Christ, and spiritual guidance. Thousands of small groups in churches of many denominations, including tens of thousands of participants, have experienced *Companions in Christ.*

After the launch of *Companions in Christ*, work began on a parallel resource for children. In 2006 *The Way of the Child* met with immediate acceptance and praise. Developed by Christian educator Wynn McGregor, this experiential resource on spirituality leads children into a life of prayer, Bible reading, worship, and service in the name of Christ. A parallel resource for youth,

This child traces a finger labyrinth while praying at the Gazing reflection station.

At right, a young girl rakes sand as she thinks about the Bible story presented earlier in the large-group Conversation portion of the session.

The Upper Room staff in December 2008—**Row 1:** Alpina Lopez, Theresa Santillan, Marcela Castelan, Rhonda Moore, Ruth Moredock, Marilyn Beaty, Melanie Hooper, Alma Pérez. **Row 2:** Sherry Elliott, Gerrie Grimsley, Metral Smith, Mary Milam Granberry, Alma Swinney, Janice King, Frances Rivera, Terrie Livaudais, Edna Vaughan, Mary Gregory, Beth Richardson, Lynn Gilliam, Steve Bryant. **Row 3:** Charlene Eubank, JoAnn Miller, Patty McIntyre, Kimberly Jenkins, Teresa Flemmings, Cynthia Johnson, Carmen Gaud, Nicole Corlew, Laura Feliciano-Esperanza, Mirza Esteban, Pattie Jones, Migdiel Pérez. **Row 4:** Victor Pérez, Donna Bryant, Joane Pettus, Deana Frederick, Tim Barnett, Cynthia Smith, George Donigian, Debbie Gregory, Jeannie Crawford-Lee, Melissa Tidwell, Rita Collett, Kathleen Stephens, Cindy Helms. **Row 5:** Nanci Lamar, Greg Engroff, Chris McCormick, Patricia Mundy, Lynne Deming, Marjorie Thompson, Patricia Olds, Cynthia Begnaud, Jorge Berrios, Sandy Miller, Susan King, Jamie Abernathy. **Row 6:** Tom Albin, Jeff Runyan, Robin Pippin, Doug Hagler, Kathryn Kimball, John Mogabgab, Rebecca West, Anne Trudel, Janice Rosson, Patrick Bass, Jim Stafford, Mary Linda Morgan, Shawana Brown, Jerry Haas.

Marcia McFee, Stephen Bryant, and Marjorie Thompson prepare for a Communion service at SOULfeast 2008.

Looking toward the worship platform in the open-air auditorium at Lake Junaluska, North Carolina (SOULfeast 2008)

The Way of Pilgrimage, was introduced in 2007. Like the resource for adults, the youth resource focuses on the central disciplines of the Christian journey.

The adult Companions in Christ series includes additional modules for small groups: *Exploring the Way, The Way of Blessedness, The Way of Forgiveness, The Way of Transforming Discipleship, The Way of Grace, The Way of Prayer*, and *The Way of Discernment.*

Upper Room Customer Service representative Patricia Olds sings with worship leader Marcia McFee.

TENDING SOULS

As thousands of people experience God's shaping power through these resources, The Upper Room has become increasingly identified with a contemplative approach to spiritual formation and to the Christian life. Our hectic culture leaves people deeply weary, and contemplative spirituality offers a place of equally deep rest. Leaders want to learn more about this approach in order to introduce it and model it in their congregations. SOULfeast, a gathering held at Lake Junaluska, North Carolina, began as an experiment in 2004 and offers Bible teaching, inspiring worship, and practical training in spirituality for leaders and groups. Participants responded the first year by asking that SOULfeast be an annual event.

But not everyone who was interested could travel to the Southeast to attend the conference. By 2006, a group from Texas asked The Upper Room to offer a similar event there, calling it SOULfiesta and making it even more of a congregational program. The next year, SOULfiesta moved to Arizona. By 2008 these relationships evolved into a multiyear relationship between The Upper Room and churches in the Desert Southwest Conference of The United Methodist Church.

A VISION OF MUTUAL MINISTRY

In 2008 The Upper Room launched Pray with Africa, a new program reflecting the mutuality that increasingly characterizes our ministry. We often hear requests

In 2008 Pray with Africa became The Upper Room's latest expression of ministry in Africa. It emphasizes praying *with* our brothers and sisters in Africa, a mutual ministry.

The Pray with Africa (USA) staff: Cary Graham, director; Austin Flack, videographer; Ciona Rouse, writer.

to pray *for* some other group or country, but Pray with Africa focuses on mutual ministry. We work alongside our brothers and sisters in all parts of Africa, learning from one another. The worldwide community of prayer engendered by *The Upper Room* magazine continues to draw people together across oceans and continents. We are eager to see where God will take us next.

Decade Highlights

2001

Companions in Christ, MethodX.net, and MP3 audio version of *The Upper Room* are launched.

2002

Africa Portuguese edition begins. Africa Upper Room Ministries opens Anathoth.

2004

Discussion questions for small groups are introduced in *The Upper Room*. Africa French radio edition is launched.

2005

Prayers for Encouragement is published for people living with HIV/AIDS and other serious illnesses.

2006

The Way of the Child is launched.

2007

The Way of Pilgrimage is introduced.

2008

Daily meditations from *The Upper Room* are broadcast in Africa in Kiswahili and IsiZulu. Launch of Pray with Africa. Russian edition begins publication.

The Upper Room

Epilogue: Still Listening

As the first decade of the twenty-first century has unfolded, electronic media have changed rapidly. The emerging technology seen in personal recording devices and electronic readers will transform the way people read. Like everyone else in industrial cultures, we face the challenge of adapting our products and ways of delivering them to customers. As in earlier decades, The Upper Room will use these challenges to expand our ministry.

The unfolding ministry of *The Upper Room* over these 75 years has been amazing. It still is and always has been about people—about the more than 25,000 who have written for the magazine, about the countless millions around the world who have read their witness of God's unfailing love and grace.

But this ministry happened only because people listened to one another and risked failure. Church people of the 1930s listened to the dream that Frances Craig and Grover Emmons carried in their hearts—the dream of a devotional magazine that would appeal to and speak to all kinds of people. In every decade since, leaders of The Upper Room's ministries have repeatedly demonstrated willingness to listen to God's dreams as they emerge through the words of God's people. This has been the strength and the growing edge of the ministry.

We don't know what is next, but God does. God goes before us, always opening doors. Our part is to follow. As we listen to what God is saying to and through God's people around the world, we expect to hear the Spirit calling and leading us into new areas of ministry.

What are you hearing from God? What is the next vision that we need to attend to? We invite you to tell us. We're listening.

About the Author

Mary Lou Redding joined the staff as managing editor of *The Upper Room* daily devotional guide in 1979. In her current position as editorial director, she leads retreats and writers' workshops in the United States and abroad. Her writings have appeared in numerous magazines, including *Alive Now, Weavings, Christian Writer,* and *Solo.*

She is the author of several Upper Room books: *Meeting God in Scripture: Entering the Old Testament*, *The Power of a Focused Heart: 8 Life Lessons from the Beatitudes*, *While We Wait: Living the Questions of Advent*, and *Breaking and Mending: Divorce and God's Grace*. Mary Lou also contributed to *The Spiritual Formation Bible* that The Upper Room copublished with Zondervan.

Mary Lou holds a BA in English Literature from Oral Roberts University and an MA in Rhetoric and Writing from the University of Tulsa. She has pursued further study at Vanderbilt Divinity School and completed the two-year Academy for Spiritual Formation offered by The Upper Room.

Mary Lou has one adult daughter, Lisa, and one granddaughter, Rosalie. She loves word games and is an Atlanta Braves fan.

The staff of *The Upper Room*—Jim Stafford, associate editor; Marilyn Beaty, editorial assistant; Susan King, assistant editor; and Mary Lou Redding, editorial director.

The staff of *El Aposento Alto*—Carmen Gaud, international editor; Jorge Berrios, associate editor; and Theresa Santillan, editorial assistant.

The Upper Room, 2009

www.ingramcontent.com/pod-product-compliance
Lightning Source LLC
LaVergne TN
LVHW071144251025
824244LV00011B/2